DISPUTED WATERS

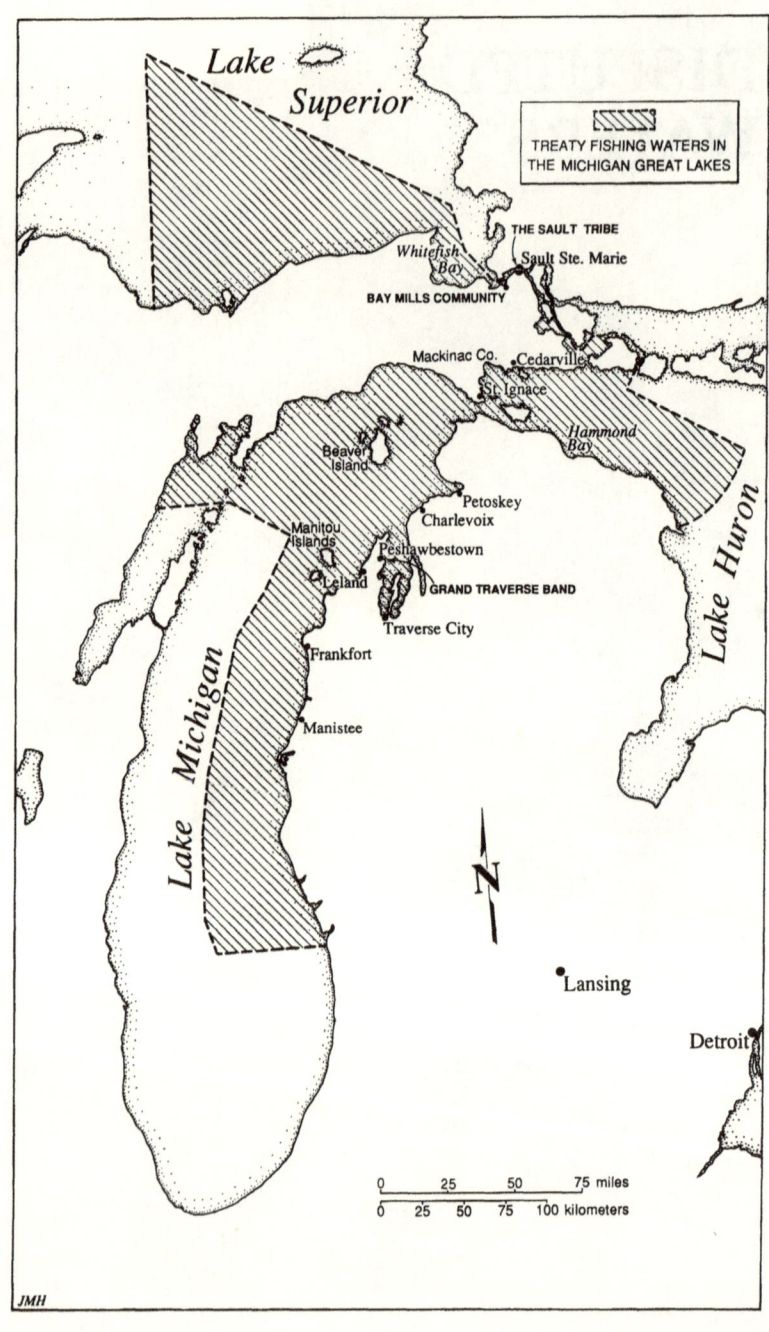

DISPUTED WATERS

Native Americans and the Great Lakes Fishery

ROBERT DOHERTY

THE UNIVERSITY PRESS OF KENTUCKY

Frontispiece: Treaty Fishing Waters in the Michigan Great Lakes

Copyright © 1990 by The University Press of Kentucky
Scholarly publisher for the Commonwealth,
serving Bellarmine College, Berea College, Centre
College of Kentucky, Eastern Kentucky University,
The Filson Club, Georgetown College, Kentucky
Historical Society, Kentucky State University,
Morehead State University, Murray State University,
Northern Kentucky University, Transylvania University,
University of Kentucky, University of Louisville,
and Western Kentucky University.

Editorial and Sales Offices: Lexington, Kentucky 40506-0336

Library of Congress Cataloging-in-Publication Data
Doherty, Robert, 1935-
  Disputed waters : Native Americans and the Great Lakes fishery / Robert Doherty.
    p. cm.
  Includes bibliographical references and index.
  ISBN 978-0-8131-5206-6 (acid-free paper)
  1. Ojibwa Indians—Water rights. 2. Ottawa Indians—Water rights. 3. Ojibwa Indians—Fishing—Law and legislation. 4. Ottawa Indians—Fishing—Law and legislation. 5. Ojibwa Indians—Government relations. 6. Ottawa Indians—Government relations. I. Title.
E99.C6D64 1990
333.2—dc20   90-39198

This book is printed on acid-free paper meeting
the requirements of the American National Standard
for Permanence of Paper for Printed Library Materials. ∞

Contents

Preface   vii

Introduction: Rights, Resource Allocation, and the Fishery   1

1. The Fur Trade   7
2. The Great Lakes Fishery, 1836-1965   23
3. Social Structure and the Forests   38
4. Tourism and Sport Fishing   51
5. Chippewa and Ottawa Treaty Rights   67
6. Treaty Rights in the Courts   86
7. State Efforts to Regain Control   105
8. With Utmost Good Faith?   124
9. What Should Be Done?   140

Epilogue   152

Notes   156

Index   169

Preface

I spent ten summers in northern Michigan researching *Disputed Waters*. I love this region where, long ago, my Irish immigrant grandfather established his American home. When I told my eighty-year-old father about this book and the wholesale fish business I had begun, he seemed bemused, "Your grandad," he smiled, "would be proud. In the old days, when I was a boy, he bought fish from the Indians for his meat market in Petoskey." As if welcoming back one of their own, local residents opened their homes and offices to me when I called and inquired about "Indian fishing." They patiently answered my questions, often providing new insights and information. My thanks to: William P. Horn, Gordon and Emma Peterson, Sharon Morin, James Olson, Helen Tanner, Dean Robb, Arthur LeBlanc, Albert LeBlanc, Joseph Lumsden, John Alexander, Arthur Duhamel, Ron Paquin, Barry Levine, Nancy Kida, Bill James, and Dan Green. Bruce R. Greene was especially helpful during the early stages of my research. And I found his impeccable legal skills inspiring.

William Rastetter, attorney for the Grand Traverse band, helped me more than anyone else. He allowed me to use his notes, showed me correspondence among *United States* v. *Michigan* litigants, and talked with me at length about the case. We became friends and he hired me to prepare myself to testify in federal court as an expert witness on the band's behalf. Despite accepting money from the band, I do not consider myself to be either its advocate or the advocate of any other party to the suit.

Though I did most of my research on the scene, watching

events unfold and interviewing participants, I also spent many hours in several libraries. The staffs in the Michigan State Archives, Bayliss Library, Traverse City Public Library, Northwestern Michigan College Library, University of Pittsburgh Library, and the National Indian Law Library patiently assisted me, often locating material I might never have found on my own.

Ed Symons talked with me about the legal chapters and suggested several productive lines of argument. Grace Tomcho typed the manuscript and cheerfully made revisions. Judith Bailey skillfully edited my prose, improving it without violating my meaning. Evalin Douglas and William Jerome Crouch of the University Press of Kentucky have been gracious and supportive. I especially appreciate Jerome Crouch's directness and his selection of helpfully critical readers, one of whom was Robert W. Venables.

The virtues of the book thus derive from many sources; its flaws, of course, are of my own doing.

INTRODUCTION

Rights, Resource Allocation, and the Fishery

On March 26, 1985, the leaders of three Chippewa and Ottawa bands signed an agreement with the United States and the state of Michigan that recognized their exclusive rights to net fish in northern Lakes Michigan and Huron. Negotiated after a bitter and sometimes violent conflict between whites and Native Americans, the agreement ended, it was hoped, a 150-year-old struggle. As of the fall of 1989, a fragile peace prevailed, but the dispute simmered on, threatening to boil over at any moment.

Disputed Waters examines this struggle over fishing rights as it reveals the nature of public policy making and the quality of administrative politics. The book explores how resources are allocated, how allocations are administered, and what effect recent interpretations of Native American rights have had. The issues analyzed here reach beyond fish and the Great Lakes: Should Native Americans be accorded superior rights to resources as a consequence of treaty rights and aboriginal occupancy? Are court rulings in support of Native American claims legally correct and ethically appropriate? What standards should be used to evaluate court rulings and resource allocations? To what extent have guarantees of equal rights actually promoted equal access to resources? Or has the notion of "equality" often merely justified inequalities already in place? How are public policies made? How does their administration affect resource allocations? Whose interests are served? The public's? What, in fact, is the public interest? How is it determined? By whom?

Ottawa and Chippewa Indians made Michigan their home several hundred years before whites arrived in the early 1600s. The Indians harvested the earth's bounty by farming, hunting, fishing, and gathering wild foods. White fur traders disrupted this age-old self-sufficiency and drew the Indians into a commercial network in which they worked as provisioners, craftsmen, trappers, and fishermen. Ottawa and Chippewa men earned credit and money with which they bought European goods they could not make for themselves. A new way of life blossomed for a while and Indians prospered.

Prior to the arrival of whites, the Indians had sustained themselves within a localized subsistence economy that afforded them relative security and a chance to nourish their spiritual and emotional needs. This was no Eden populated by noble savages, even though these hunters and gatherers lived within supportive communities as free, independent people. But white men drew the Chippewas and Ottawas into a market system that destroyed this self-sufficient and autonomous way of life. In the long run, the market and its supporting institutions created an economy in which the Indians gained little success. Today, the Chippewas and Ottawas of upper Michigan struggle in an economy largely irrelevant to their needs, which serves the summertime pleasures of non-Indians who vacation in the area but live far away.

The Chippewas and Ottawas had efficiently met their needs before non-Indian fur traders and government officials imposed market-based ideas and institutions, which clashed with the Indians' ideals and practices. The Native Americans had generously shared more abundant resources, such as fish, among themselves and with strangers, giving with an easy generosity that shocked outsiders. But the Indians carefully distributed scarce and essential resources—winter hunting grounds, for example—by allocating territorial harvest rights to extended families. Allocation did not convey fee simple ownership but merely extended usufructuary rights and obligations that ceased when they were not exercised. Furthermore, the resources themselves were to be granted ethical consideration.[1]

Non-Indians little understood native attitudes and practices, which, in any case, ill suited the fur traders, lumbermen, and fishermen who came to the region seeking profits and who viewed animals, trees, and fish as mere commodities. Once in control, these newcomers put in place a system that opened access to the resources of upper Michigan to anyone who wished to take them. Ownership resulted from capture—trapping an animal or catching a fish—and included rights to dispose of the resource in any way the captor wished. Open access and the rule of capture held sway for several generations, eventually coming to seem *given*, ordained by some natural order, rather than devised by human invention.[2]

Environmental disasters soon followed. This new profit-centered system encouraged exploitation without regard for non-economic constraints. So lumbermen cut too many trees, hunters and trappers killed too many animals, and fishermen netted too many fish. Supplies dwindled. Profits disappeared. People moved away.

Upper Michigan had no market for the large supplies of lumber, fur, meat, and fish produced during the early years of exploitation. These products were shipped to larger markets—Chicago, Detroit, Buffalo, New York City, and elsewhere—for eventual sale. The spin-off benefits fell to urban dwellers, who obtained both the use of the resources and the secondary profits from them. As a consequence, northern Michigan developed a rather simple economy built on the export of natural resources.

Successful participation in this export economy demanded capital and market savvy, neither of which the Native Americans possessed in abundance. Some Chippewas and Ottawas became entrepreneurs for a while, but most took wage-earning jobs that offered limited opportunities for advancement but allowed some independence from government handouts.

By the 1870s, trapping, habitat destruction, and market hunting had decimated animal populations, and within a few years lumbermen had removed most of the usable timber. Upper Michigan became a cutover wasteland, its sparse population reduced to poverty. Great Lakes commercial fishing survived precariously until the 1950s because the lakes had initially contained such a variety of marketable species. The fishermen were able to switch to a new target species whenever they used up the previous one. In the 1960s, however, the fishery collapsed spectacularly. Formerly productive waters now teemed with alewives, suitable only for fertilizer. Few commercially valuable edible fish survived.[3]

The state of Michigan began to protect game animals in 1881 by enacting hunting laws that imposed bag limits, controlled seasons, and restricted market hunting. The state started to restore its forests in the 1920s. But with its resources for export mostly used up, the region slid into economic distress for which widespread relief seemed unavailable until the rise of mass tourism in the 1950s.

With beautiful beaches, lakes, and streams, and cool, sunny weather, northern Michigan well suited the summer tourist trade. Upper-class vacationers had enjoyed the region as early as the late nineteenth century, but large numbers of middle-class visitors began coming to the area only in the 1950s in the wake of widespread prosperity and rising personal incomes. Many Americans now had discretionary income to spend on leisure and outdoor recreation. The family vacation became an expected part of middle-class life.

Clearly, tourism was going to become a booming industry. Michigan state officials quickly recognized its potential and seized upon tourism as a cure for north-country economic woes and as a stimulus to the sagging economy of the entire state, dragged down by the decline in automobile manufacturing. Tourism altered upper Michigan and brought prosperity of a sort, but it disrupted older ways of life and seldom helped longtime residents find economic security.

To encourage tourism and to make its northern regions both accessible and appealing the state created several programs: advertising and promotion, tourist information services, new four-lane highways and improved public facilities, upgraded state parks and campgrounds, public boat-launching sites, enhanced hunting and fishing opportunities, environmental protection. The most spectacular and widely publicized of these programs restored the Great Lakes fishery, curbed commercial netting, and allocated newly stocked lake trout and salmon to sports anglers. Within a few years, the Michigan Great Lakes had become world-class sport-fishing waters.

The rejuvenated fishery ran headlong into a rising Native American consciousness and Chippewa and Ottawa claims of aboriginal rights to Great Lakes fish that superseded state authority. Beginning in the early 1970s, Native American fishermen began testing the limits of state power by netting whitefish and lake trout contrary to state regulations, engaging in what the news media called "fish-ins." After several ensuing court cases, the Chippewas and Ottawas eventually won favorable decisions in the Michigan State Supreme Court and in the United States District Court. But despite a 1985 allocation of fish between the state and the Native Americans, conflicts over the fishery continue.

The struggle to control Great Lakes fish was ugly from the outset. Indian claims threatened to overturn well-established social arrangements that ensured white dominance. "Treaty fishing," as the Chippewas and Ottawas called it, gave the Native Americans a cause around which to rally as they sought to reestablish historic rights. To many whites, Indian claims seemed unbelievable and ill founded, based as they were upon documents signed a century or more in the past. How could such old papers accord rights to Native Americans that were denied to everyone else? Shouldn't everyone be equal?

Infuriated, some non-Indians equated Native American rights with affirmative-action programs.

White sport fishermen and Indian netters confronted one another on the beaches and the lakes. Although they were usually content with verbal assaults, the sportsmen often destroyed Native American boats and fishing gear, threatened to injure native fishermen, and tried to intimidate them with night-riding vigilantism. Anonymous callers threatened to burn out businesses that bought and sold Indian-caught fish. Contending that tragedy would ensue if state control were not promptly restored, the governor of Michigan heated up the struggle by issuing dark warnings about violence, environmental disaster, and financial loss. But the Chippewas and Ottawas refused to back down.

CHAPTER ONE
The Fur Trade

Chippewa and Ottawa Indians entered the fur trade in the mid–seventeenth century, shortly after white men first arrived in upper Michigan. Chippewas remained active in the trade until treaty-signing times in the 1830s, but the Ottawas ceased participating directly when they migrated to lower Michigan in the mid–eighteenth century, cut back their trapping, and became food suppliers. They continued that involvement into the early nineteenth century.

Frenchmen controlled the fur trade in the region until their military defeat in 1760. They maintained easygoing and tolerant relationships with the Chippewas and Ottawas and often took Indian wives. Mixed-bloods soon began to play important roles in the fur business. Even French missionaries, though bent upon converting the Indians to Catholicism, appear to have respected native cultures.[1]

The French did entice the Indians into European diplomatic and military conflicts. Chippewas and Ottawas fought in wars that took place hundreds of miles from their homes and involved non-Indian, European-centered issues. French missions and forts rearranged older settlement patterns, and the fur trade altered the annual round of subsistence activities. In short, the French provoked extraordinary changes in the lives of the Chippewa and Ottawa Indians, who nevertheless appear to have adapted successfully while retaining substantial control over their lives.[2]

American traders, who took over in the early nineteenth century after a few years of British control, tolerated Indian differences from themselves much less than the French had. They cultivated neither friendship nor trade with the Indians, though as middlemen and trappers, the Indians were the source of furs. The Americans brought broader economic interests than the French or even the British, both of whom had concentrated on the fur trade and made few efforts to develop other resources or possess the land. The Indians had useful functions in the French-British system as trappers, provisioners, and traders, but the Americans wanted to settle, to develop, to take control. Ultimately, they wanted to own everything, including the land and its resources. In 1836 they forced the Indians to sign a treaty that dispossessed the Chippewas and Ottawas of all but some tiny reservations.[3]

In 1820 Michigan territorial governor and soon-to-be secretary of war Lewis Cass embarked on a federally sponsored exploratory expedition from Mackinac to Sault Ste. Marie, along the south shore of Lake Superior and inland to the headwaters of the Mississippi. Several members of the expedition published letters and reports that hawked the economic potential of the region, especially mining, lumbering, and fishing. Significantly, before the trip even got under way, Cass persuaded the L'Arbre Croche bands to sell the St. Martin Islands in the Mackinac Straits to the United States, so that the Americans could begin mining gypsum there. Cass negotiated a second land-cession treaty in Sault Ste. Marie, where he bought land on which to build a military post. Cass, purchased only a small plot "because it [was] important to our character and influence among them, that our first demand should be distinctly marked with moderation."[4]

As word of the economic possibilities spread, the fisheries attracted immediate attention. Henry R. Schoolcraft's widely circulated *Narrative Journal* praised the Great Lakes fishery and made clear that a teeming abundance of whitefish, sturgeon, and lake trout lay waiting for commercial exploitation. In 1832 Americans began to reorganize the fishery in the Mackinac

The Fur Trade 9

Straits, curbing Indian fishing and beginning to sell fish outside the region. These were ominous changes, since the Chippewas and Ottawas needed the fish for food.

Apparently, the Americans also introduced a priggish morality and a racism and classism that discriminated against Indians and mixed-bloods and limited their chances for advancement. Indian agent Henry R. Schoolcraft, who held sway in the Mackinac region between 1822 and 1842, was a narrow-minded and ethnocentric Calvinist. Working through the Presbyterian church, Schoolcraft tried to foster a revival of religion, decency, and proper social arrangements in a society he felt had lost itself in materialism and debauchery.[5]

Wanting both to assimilate and to remain autonomous, Catholic Ottawas from L'Arbre Croche sought to interpose their church between themselves and Schoolcraft's schemes. Ottawa leaders invited the church to assign them a priest and renew its mission among them. The Indians sent three gifted Ottawa youngsters to a Catholic seminary in Cincinnati. In 1829 the two boys, Augustin Hamlin, Jr., and William Blackbird, went on to Rome to finish their education while the girl, Margaret Blackbird, remained at the Ohio school. Ottawa plans to use these well-trained young leaders and the Catholic mission as a buffer against American ambitions ultimately failed to control the newcomers and to preserve native independence, though they undoubtedly helped the Ottawas avoid a full-scale uprooting from their homeland and removal to the West.[6]

Not content with religious and political reactions to white encroachments, the Indians also tried to alter the economic system—especially resource ownership—to preserve their independence. White visitors among Chippewa and Ottawa bands found the Indians' generosity impressive. Visiting in 1695, Antoine de la Mothe Cadillac commented that Ottawa hunters profited least by their hunting, since they gave away the meat from the animals they had killed:

They often make feasts for their friends or relations or distribute the animals they have killed. . . . One proof of the liberality of the vanity which they acquire from this occupation is that, when they land at their village, the persons present . . . are permitted to take and carry off all the meat in the canoe of the hunter who has killed it, and he does nothing but laugh. That is sufficient reason for believing that their only idea is to feed the people; and as the whole tribe feels the benefit of this, it is interested in praising such a noble calling, especially as it often happens that a single hunter provides food for several families which, but for his aid would, at certain times and at certain places, perish of hunger and want.[7]

Gift giving, sharing, and generosity ensured a relatively secure subsistence in a localized economy based upon seasonal migrations to harvest abundant resources: scarcity and abundance were spread around. The market system, however, which commercialized resources, threatened the ability of the Chippewas and Ottawas to feed themselves. The Indians adjusted their former ways, trying insofar as possible to secure their food supplies. They allocated hunting territories to specific families and fought the fur company's later efforts to monopolize fishing grounds. And they complained generally about non-Indians who encroached upon their resources. Chippewas and Ottawas had not suddenly become thick-skinned and selfish. They merely wished to survive.

The Ottawa and Chippewa Indians of northern Michigan depended on fishing as their major food source. This was the case in the early nineteenth century during treaty times just as it had been for centuries preceding white dominance. During spring and fall, when the fish crowded into shallow water, the Indians caught them by the thousands. Without Great Lakes fish, the existence of the Ottawa and Chippewa peoples would have been completely different. Certainly they could not have lived together in large groups without fish, for other food sources were too scarce to have supported many people in one place at one time.

In order to use the sparse resources of the north woods

The Fur Trade

efficiently, members of the Ottawa and Chippewa bands migrated seasonally to locations where they could find adequate resources. In time, these movements settled into well-established patterns, an annual round. The pattern varied from place to place, depending on the flora and fauna and the amount of farming practiced by a band or a group, but its basic rhythms remained. From late spring through early fall, the Ottawas and Chippewas lived in relatively large groups on the shores of the Great Lakes, where fish provided plenty to eat. Ottawas from L'Arbre Croche also farmed during the summer. In the fall, these large gatherings separated into smaller kin-linked groups of a dozen or so people, leaving the Great Lakes coast and migrating to family hunting grounds usually located about fifty miles inland along the banks of a river.

Corn-raising Indians, farmers such as the Ottawas who occupied lands near L'Arbre Croche in 1742, developed an annual round that focused more on their semisedentary agricultural settlements than on fishing villages. Women tended the fields during the summer and remained in the settlements while the men went off to hunt. Nevertheless, the settlements split into smaller units when the families went to their winter hunting grounds. Seasonal migrations remained important to the L'Arbre Croche Ottawas until the 1840s and possibly beyond that time.[8]

John Tanner, a white man who lived among the Ottawas during the early nineteenth century, described his family's winter trek from Mackinac: "The corn was ripe when we reached that place, and after stopping a little while, we went three days up the river to the place where they intended to pass the winter. We then left our canoes, and travelling over the land, camped three times before we came to the place where we set up our lodges for the winter."[9] Tanner and his Indian family wintered in the same spot the following year, and they survived this difficult season with relative ease.

In the early nineteenth century, most Indians spent their winters in these inland camps, hunting and trapping for food (fur trapping was no longer profitable). The same families appear to have used the same winter camps year after year and had developed a sense of ownership—probably feeling that the right to use the resources near the camp belonged to them. These family camps lay scattered along Michigan rivers. Some families traveled far from their summer grounds to winter camp in the southern part of the lower peninsula, where more game could be found among deciduous forests. Ottawa families from L'Arbre Croche, for example, wintered far to the south along the Muskegon River.[10]

The families left these hunting camps in late winter and went to the maple groves, the coast, and the fishing grounds. Maple sap ordinarily became available before the fish; so the families camped first among the sugar bush. Larger than the winter camps, sugaring groups involved several related families, who lived near one another while harvesting the sap. Often these people had wintered in separate family-based camps along the same watershed but now came together to enjoy the spring bounty.

When the flow of maple sap waned, the families moved to their fishing camps. Gathered now in large groups—a band of several extended families—the Indians fished and gathered wild edibles; some farmed. These large groups persisted through the summer and early fall until the annual round began once more and the people separated into small family units for their trek to the winter hunting camps.

These migratory customs of the Ottawas and Chippewas defined a system for owning and allocating resources, described in a detailed eyewitness account written by a careful observer, Alexander Henry, a British fur trader born in New Jersey. Henry arrived in northern Michigan in the late summer of 1762—a few months before the British took over the area from its French occupants. Interested in entering the fur trade, Henry began contacting members of the Ottawa and Chippewa bands of northern Michigan. He was captured by Chippewa Indians when they seized the fort at Mackinac and

The Fur Trade 13

probably would have been killed if his Chippewa friend Chief Wawatam had not rescued him.

Henry spent the winter of 1763-64 with Chief Wawatam and his immediate family. They camped along a river that flows into Lake Michigan about 150 miles south of Mackinac, which Henry calls the Aux Sables. (Obviously it was not the river now known as the Au Sable, which flows into Lake Huron, but was probably the modern Pere Marquette or Big Sable in Mason County). Henry and Wawatam's family moved upstream about seventy miles from Lake Michigan before they made their camp. Henry says, "At our wintering-ground we were to be alone, for the Indian families, in the countries of which I write, separate in the winter season, and reassociate in the spring and summer."[11]

In the spring of 1764 Henry and the family left the winter camp and went to a sugar grove near the shore of Lake Michigan. Henry described the situation: "Arrived here, we turned our attention to sugar-making, the management of which . . . belongs to the women, the men cutting wood for the fires, and hunting and fishing. In the midst of this, we were joined by several lodges of Indians, most of whom were of the family to which I belonged, and had wintered near us. The lands belonged to this family, and it had therefore the exclusive right to hunt on them. This is according to the custom of the people; for each family has its own lands."[12]

Henry's choice of words here seems important, especially "own" and "exclusive right." We might wish that Henry had told us more about how goods were allocated among the Ottawas and Chippewas—whether such other resources as berry patches, cornfields, and fishing grounds "belonged" to certain families, who had an "exclusive right" to them.

What does the word *ownership* mean from the standpoint of Ottawa-Chippewa culture? Certainly it cannot be equated with the white system of individual possession in fee simple, including rights to lease or sell property. Among the Indians, ownership was vested in a group, which owned harvest rights through traditional use. Ownership ceased when the harvest rights were not used, and although the Ottawa and Chippewa bands had a well-developed sense of territoriality, the land itself was not owned. The leading expert on Indian land-tenure systems believes that "all Indian peoples recognized bounds to their use of the environment and mobility within it, and, whether as a corporate entity (e.g., tribe), or as a smaller socioeconomic group (e.g., band), to our knowledge all Indians allocated resources of their environment among their own kind."[13]

Tradition held such systems together. Under ordinary circumstances, the participants were largely unaware of the existence of a system at all. Year after year, they did as they had always done, moving from place to place, harvesting resources. The system came into play and people became aware of it only when something changed: resources became scarce or valuable in some new way; outsiders trespassed and harvested resources where they had no right to do so.[14]

Alexander Henry describes a system of allocation in which the Ottawa and Chippewa Indians assigned the right to exploit a resource (for example, wild animals or sugar bush) in a specified territory to a certain group. The accuracy of Henry's descriptions is confirmed by those of other observers. Seventy-five years after Henry wrote his account, Johann Kohl visited upper Michigan and described similar allocations. Since Kohl's account was written in the late 1850s, it would seem that the Ottawa and Chippewa system of allocating common resources remained in place through the period of treaty making, 1820-1855:

The beaver dams—so persons conversant with the subject assured me—all have owners among the Indians, and are handed down from father to son. The sugar camps, or "sucreries," as the Canadians call them, have all an owner, and no Indian family would think of making sugar at a place where it had no right. Even the cranberry patches, or places in the swamp and bush where that berry is plucked, are family property; and the same with many other things. If this be so, and has

The Fur Trade

been so, as seems very probable, since time immemorial, we can easily imagine how the irruption of the white men into their country must have been a tremendous insult and infringement of law in the eyes of the Indians.[15]

Ruth Landes points to the logic of such allocation systems. She notes that goods in short supply and those important to survival (for example, winter meat) were carefully apportioned, whereas ownership of more readily available goods (for example, fish) was lax. It is when goods became scarce or commercially valuable, Landes contends, that disputes over ownership arose.[16]

Among the Ottawas and Chippewas, the band—a group of extended families identified with a specific locale—was the center of the allocation system. This is to be expected, since the band was the most important unit in the lives of these Indians during the early nineteenth century. The Indian tribes and nations that we often read about were created by whites and had little impact on day-to-day Indian life. During the early nineteenth century, the band held sway over its members to the extent that it owned resources and apportioned them among its constituent families.

Government officials recognized the significance of the band before and during the period of treaty making. Indian agents regularly identified their charges by band, usually referring to the location of the group's summer home territory: Cheboigan Chenos (Les Cheneaux), L'Arbre Croche, and so forth. In 1819, when agent George Boyd reported on the condition of the Indians within the Agency of Michilimackinac, he described his charges band by band, noting the differences among them. Whites negotiated treaties with band leaders, and Indian signatories were identified by band affiliation. When the chiefs and headmen petitioned President Andrew Jackson in 1835, they identified themselves by band. Leaders signed from Chenos, Oak Point, St. Martin, St. Mary's, St. Ignace, Mackinac, Cheboigan, Epouvetts, Upper and Lower L'Arbre Croche, Lake Michigan, and Little Traverse. Recognition by whites simply reflects the importance of the bands among the Indians.[17]

The Chippewa and Ottawa bands of the early nineteenth century owned the common goods on which their members subsisted. The word *owned* here connotes usufructuary ownership: they owned the right to harvest wild animals, fruits of the land, and fish. The band apportioned this general right among its members by assigning to families and groups of families "territory" in which they harvested common goods. The right to take the scarcest and most crucial goods—animals for winter hunting—was assigned to small groups as an exclusive right to harvest game within a specified territory. Rights to more abundant goods, maple sugar and fish, for example, were assigned to larger groups on a less exclusive basis. But the basic system of *band ownership and assignment of group rights to harvest goods within a given territory* remains consistent.

Family hunting territories grew out of scarcity as a way to increase efficiency and decrease competition for food. Alexander Henry's description of his winter with the Ottawas emphasizes the hunting territory as a place to get food, especially deer, but not fur bearers, though Henry seems generally preoccupied with keeping his stomach well filled, more concerned than most Indians probably would have been. These concerns did not exist with regard to fish, however. Fish could be readily caught, spring through fall, and no one worried much about who caught them where. Nevertheless, we should not be misled; the bands had strong interests in the grounds upon which they and their ancestors had fished. They moved quickly to protect those interests when whites threatened them.

Indians fished the same grounds and used the same camps for hundreds of years before whites arrived in northern Michigan. Anthropologists who have excavated these fishing camps have discovered layer on layer of fish bones, indicating use over several centuries. When the Indian bands sold their lands

The Fur Trade   17

to the United States in 1836, they retained lands on which they planned to live. Typically, band leaders chose to retain property near the fishing ground the band members customarily used. We do not know with certainty the reasons for these choices, but we can infer that fish were a crucial resource and that the bands were expressing an interest in, a sense of owning, their customary fishing grounds. In cases when access to the grounds had been threatened, as it was on the north shore of Lake Michigan, the band leaders made sure that the treaty creating onshore reservations also reserved the fishing grounds for their use.[18]

Members of the Sault band negotiated a treaty with the United States in 1820, giving up sixteen square miles of land along the St. Mary's River near its famed whitefish grounds. But the band reserved both a place to camp and the fishing grounds. The United States soon built Fort Brady on the ceded land. The white occupants of the fort and other whites in the small village there trespassed on Sault land and caught fish on the band's whitefish grounds. Members of the band complained to Francis Audrain, the Indian agent at the Sault. Audrain wrote to Henry Schoolcraft on June 13, 1833, describing how Shingwak and Kawquash and about twenty-five followers had visited him: "Shangwak and Kawquash made speeches, the tenor of which were complaints against the white people for building houses and fishing on the reservation." Two years later Schoolcraft wrote to the commander at Fort Brady and recommended that the Indians of St. Mary's sell some of their land so that the Indians might have a blacksmith shop. "This course would rid us of the complaints of the Indians for trespass on their lands and would also permit the citizens of the straits of St. Mary's to occupy without license the fishing grounds, for which they have (within the last year) been so clamorous."[19]

The Treaty of 1820 had been negotiated with the Sault band only, and Schoolcraft assumed that members of the band could grant whites access to the St. Mary's fishing grounds. More important, it was the leaders of the local band who protested about whites trespassing on their fishing grounds. Members of other bands were apparently unconcerned, since we have no evidence of protest from them. Their grounds were not being violated, and so they did not object.

Whites consistently trespassed on the encampment the Sault band had reserved along the St. Mary's River. Both the encampment and the fishing grounds were badly damaged by canal construction in 1853. Members of the Sault band requested compensation, which they were granted in a separate treaty of August 2, 1855, though it was never paid. Other legal and equitable claims had been settled in the treaty of July 31, 1855, "excepting the right of fishing and encampment secured to the Chippewas of Sault Ste. Marie by the treaty of June 16, 1820."[20]

The point here is that only members of the Sault band protested about the St. Mary's grounds and that only they were to be compensated for damages. Apparently, both whites and Indians recognized ownership of the camp and fishing grounds by the Sault band and a lack of interest or ownership by other bands. Band leaders quickly protested when they felt that their interests were being violated, and the records of the Sault and Mackinac Indian agency contain many complaints by Indians about white intrusions into their land—usually illegal timber cutting. Yet only the Sault band complained about the St. Mary's fishery. Its exclusive interest may be taken as strong evidence of ownership.

There is further indication of band ownership of fishing grounds. In 1832 two employees of the American Fur Company, John A. Drew and Edward Biddle, sought to gain exclusive rights for the company to fish the grounds between the Mille Coquin and Carp rivers. Biddle and Drew paid an Indian named Nabanoi for these rights and then used their excellent political connections in Washington and Philadelphia to gain a qualified approval for their actions from the federal government. Indian Commissioner Elbert Herring encouraged

Henry Schoolcraft to recognize the fur company's fishing rights, but in the spring of 1833 Indians and French-Indians from Mackinac petitioned Schoolcraft to help them retain their right to fish the grounds near the Mille Coquin. A delegation of Ottawa and Chippewa Indians visited subagent George Johnston, Schoolcraft's brother-in-law, in Mackinac. Johnston wrote Schoolcraft that "the chiefs appeared very much incensed in Nabanoi's conduct for presuming in the first place to clothe himself with such authority, and in the second case, not making known and consulting *the real chiefs who owned the land and the fishing grounds on the said coast*" (my emphasis).[21] Again, the word *owned* seems important, used as it is by a man such as George Johnston, who was half Chippewa and experienced in Indian affairs. In any case, Indians from Little Traverse, L'Arbe Croche, St. Ignace, and Mackinac expressed an interest in the grounds claimed by Biddle and Drew. These were the chiefs who Johnston said owned the fishing grounds.

Though upset about Biddle and Drew's efforts to drive them from the Mille Coquin fishing grounds and worried about the loss of an important food source, the Chippewa and Ottawa bands did not claim exclusive rights for themselves. They did express a proprietary interest in the grounds, however. In some way, not made clear, "the chiefs who owned . . . the fishing grounds," as Johnston calls them controlled access to the grounds, and they thought that Biddle and Drew should have consulted them.

That several band leaders complained to Johnston indicates use of the grounds by native groups in the Mackinac Straits area and along the northwest coast of Michigan as far south as Little Traverse Bay. It was a pattern somewhat different from that prevailing in the Sault region, where a single band claimed the right to fish the rapids and to deny the fishery to others. In the straits area, there were many large, productive grounds, and several bands lived nearby. Therefore, the allocation system was different from that in the St. Mary's fishery, where only the rapids were productive, and the population was sparse except near the river. The two allocation systems were functional adaptations to local variations in resources and human populations.

Economic circumstances, particularly the relative scarcity or abundance of a good, shaped resource allocation among the Chippewa bands. We cannot say for certain what would have happened if fish had become scarce or commercially valuable, but there is good reason to believe the bands would have divided the fishing grounds in the same fashion they split up the hunting territories.[22]

In an article published in 1926, Frank G. Speck described the hunting territory of western Labrador and among the surrounding Algonkian bands:

> We may define the family hunting group as a kinship group composed of individuals united by blood or marriage, maintaining the right to hunt, trap and fish in a certain inherited district bounded by . . . natural landmarks. . . . with a few exceptions the whole territory claimed by each tribe was subdivided into tracts owned from time immemorial by the same families and handed down from generation to generation in the male line. The almost exact bounds of these territories were known and recognized, and trespass, which, indeed, was of rare occurrence, was summarily punishable.

Speck believed hunting territories were of aboriginal origin, not an adaptation to white contact.[23]

Subsequent research has shown that the family hunting territories were not as well defined as Speck described them. More important, it seems reasonably certain that the hunting territories were not aboriginal but developed in response to white contact, the commercialization of animals, and the fur trade. In fieldwork in Labrador in 1950, Eleanor Leacock reexamined Speck's ideas and found that hunting territories were an attempt to allocate fur-bearing animals when they acquired market value in the fur trade. Once the trade appeared, families established their territory, often blazing trees to mark its

The Fur Trade   21

boundaries. Trespass involved taking fur or meat from someone else's land, but no general concept of trespass existed. Fish were not included in this system because there was no market for them and they were abundant. Before the fur trade, Leacock notes,

> the Montagnais hunted co-operatively and shared their game, which was immediately consumed by the group. They could not preserve, store, or transport food to any great extent. Occasionally there was surplus meat to be dried and kept, but it merely filled in temporarily when hunting was poor. . . . Owing to the uncertainty of the hunt, several families were necessarily dependent on each other, thus providing "a kind of subsistence insurance or greater security than individual families could achieve." With production for trade, however, the individual's most important ties, economically speaking, were transferred from *within* the band to *without*, and his objective relation to other band members changed from the co-operative to the competitive. With storable, transportable, and individually acquired supplies . . . , the individual family became self-sufficient, and larger group living is not only superfluous in the struggle for existence but a positive hindrance to the personal acquisition of furs.[24]

Recent studies support Leacock's contention that allocation through family hunting territories arose in response to scarcity and the market system. We can be confident about the connection between commercialization and territorial division.[25]

Leacock's argument relates directly to allocation among the early nineteenth-century Ottawa and Chippewa bands. Indian bands restricted access to goods that were scarce and valuable, though not necessarily according to a market definition of the term. They adapted their systems of ownership to changing patterns of subsistence so as to use resources effectively while minimizing conflict. Given the logic of this allocation system, we would expect to find that the Chippewa and Ottawa bands allowed relatively easy access to their fishing grounds. Fish were abundant, and there was no well-organized market for them until about the late 1830s. But we can also be sure that if fish became scarce or gained value as a market developed for them, the Indian bands would allocate the fishing grounds just as they distributed the hunting territories.

CHAPTER TWO

The Great Lakes Fishery, 1836-1965

Fish taken from the upper Great Lakes became a marketable commodity when the first white people arrived in the area. Indians had swapped fish for trade goods or had just given fish to newly found white "friends." But white traders saw market opportunities.[1]

Before the whites came, Indians had maintained the fishery for thousands of years. They had fished with handcrafted gill nets from open boats. Native women worked basswood, nettle, and other natural fibers into nets, linking the strands into mesh with neatly tied sheet bends. Men fashioned cedar floats and cut grooves in small stones to be used as sinkers. They set the nets with great skill and lifted them by hand under often difficult conditions. Chippewa fishermen frequently took their canoes far offshore, where they set nets on deepwater reefs.[2]

Indians fished in the rapids of the St. Mary's River around the falls for hundreds of years. In old times, before the Sault Ste. Marie canal was built, two Indians working from a canoe could take several hundred pounds of fish in a few hours. The paddler in the stern maneuvered from rock to rock, holding the canoe in the eddies where the whitefish gathered. In the bow, the fisherman stood balanced gracefully, holding his long-handled scoop net in front of the canoe while the paddler let the craft drift slowly backward through the eddy and downstream. Pushing the net down, the netter momentarily trapped the fish, then quickly reversed the mesh and hauled his catch into the canoe.

In winter the Indians speared trout and sturgeon through the ice. The fisherman cleared away the snow, cut a hole through the ice, and built a small hut in which he could lie out of the light, hidden from the fish. Spear at ready in the clear water, watching the fish thirty or forty feet below, the fisherman lowered a small, wooden, herringlike decoy and let it swim around near the lake trout. The curious and hungry fish would move to the decoy, but as they swam closed the spearer drew his lure up until a fish came in range. Poised, muscles tense, the fisherman teased the trout under his spear and then jammed the points through its green-spotted back. Sturgeon like deepwater currents and could not be charmed to the surface like the trout; they were caught with spears that often reached forty feet in length. One man couldn't manage such an awkward weapon in flowing water; so the spearer used a helper.

In old times, the Indians also fished with small gill nets during the winter. They set their nets under the ice to catch trout and whitefish. Though less efficient than modern monofilament nets, these early gill nets of natural fiber captured many fish.

Scoop nets, spears, and small gill nets allowed the Chippewas to catch St. Mary's fish in extraordinary numbers. Elsewhere, other techniques evolved: fish traps, birch bark jacklights and spears, and large gill nets. Whatever the manner of catching them, fish sustained the native economy in the upper Great Lakes both as a source of food and as an item of trade.

The Indian gill-net fishery survived well into the twentieth century, but starting in the 1830s whites restructured the fishery. The American Fur Company organized the first large-scale commercial operation in the northern Great Lakes. The company hired French and Indian fishermen whom it took to camps along the shore of Lake Superior near well-known fishing grounds, where they fished and salted their catch. The company-owned schooner sailed by periodically to pick up barrels of preserved fish.[3]

Fur company fishermen caught enormous numbers of fish. The Lake Superior fishery had never been systematically exploited, and the outlying camps allowed the company to catch fish wherever they might be found. When fish could no longer be netted in one place, the company moved its fishermen to new camps until they found the fish again. Since the shores of the lake were unsettled in the 1840s, movement of the fishermen from one ground to another did not produce conflicts between "locals" and "outsiders." And because whitefish were so abundant, depletion—overfishing—seemed impossible. The numbers of whitefish seemed limitless. But the fur company caught so many fish that it glutted the market. Too many fish and a nationwide economic downturn spun the fur company's fish business into bankruptcy.

Despite the fur company's troubles, the economic potential of the fishery in the northern Great Lakes impressed others. During the 1840s and 1850s, English, Irish, and Scandinavian immigrants moved north and settled near the better fishing grounds. Richard Cooper, the first white settler at Harbor Springs, migrated from Genesee County, New York, in 1848 to engage in fishing. In 1851 Cooper brought a trading schooner owned by a Captain Kirtland to Harbor Springs. By this time, several other white fishermen had set up in the same port.

As experienced fishermen, Indians enthusiastically joined in this first commercial activity, though we cannot be sure just how many fished in what capacities. American Fur Company records indicate extensive involvement, primarily as wage earners but also as pieceworkers, paid for each barrel of whitefish or trout they salted. Nevertheless, the Indians' request for fish barrels in the Treaty of 1836 suggests that the Chippewas and Ottawas were fishing for themselves, not merely as employees. Missionary records confirm the existence of this independent small-boat Indian fishery. In 1846 Baptist missionary Abel Bingham commented that in Sault Ste. Marie "four young men connected with our mission have, since the opening of navigation, put up, brought to this place, and sold 105 barrels of fish, and have made preparations to enlarge business during fall fishing; . . . I visited Whitefish Point where those young men were taking fish and could not fail . . . noticing their industry."[4]. Indian agent James Ord noted in 1848 that Indians in the Sault area had marketed more than a thousand barrels of fish.[5]

Most likely, despite their apparent independence, these Indians sold their catch to the American Fur Company. No other wholesale outlets existed at that time, and the Chippewas and Ottawas lacked the business acumen to operate in Chicago and other cities. Nevertheless, it seems clear that at least a few Indians quickly and successfully adapted to the commercialization of the fishery in the 1840s. Lack of capital doomed these promising starts, however. Beginning in the 1850s, technological innovations and improved transportation revolutionized the upper Great Lakes fishery. Expensive but very efficient pound nets allowed a few big fishermen to dominate each port, and railroads enabled a small number of wholesalers to control the northern business. The introduction of power lifters in the 1890s increased big-boat dominance.

Many fishermen still hand lifted gill nets from mackinaw boats—sharp-sterned, schooner-rigged sailboats. A mackinaw boat made the deepwater fishery accessible for an investment of about three hundred dollars, including boat and equipment. But the majority of the men worked the rowboat, gill net, poor man's subsistence fishery in the onshore shallows, where a tiny investment in gear could provide food and a meager income.[6]

Economic success in the fishery—profits—depended on large investments in complex gear. Steam-driven ships cost about thirty-five hundred dollars, but their speed and dependability made them profitable. With a steamer, a few men could fish several miles of gill nets. In 1884, one Lake Superior steamer with an eight-ton capacity fished twenty miles of them.

Moving from port to port, following the fish, fishermen netted thousands of pounds of trout and whitefish. In 1871 James W. Milner noted that the "territory fished over . . . [had] increased in [Lake Michigan]. More labor, more expense, and more skill in the construction and use of nets are required now than formerly, and for the capture of a less quantity of fish."[7]

Steam tugs and nets cost so much that individual fishermen could seldom afford to own them. Hired men ran these boats; hands were paid twenty-five dollars a month and captains about twice that. Of the roughly two thousand men who fished Lake Michigan in the 1870s, slightly more than half, many of them Indians or French-Indians, labored for daily wages.

Changes in the fishery, especially increased capitalization, handicapped the Chippewas and Ottawas, and economic benefits flowed disproportionately to non-Indians. In 1883 Indian agent Edward P. Allen commented to the commissioner of Indian affairs, "There are several hundred [Indians] connected with the fisheries in our great lakes in one way or another, and a few are proprietors of fishing apparatus." Technological innovation had brought the dominance of big boats and had increased white control.[8]

The Indians had shown themselves capable of operating fish-catching businesses in the 1840s, and they performed much of the actual labor in setting pound nets and running the gill-net steamers. Indians had the requisite skills to use this new equipment, but federal officials seem never to have considered aid to upgrade Indian boats and nets. Federal policies emphasized Christianization, assimilation, and farming and made no provision for supporting economic ventures other than agriculture. The climate of northern Michigan restricted the potential of farming, however, especially in the upper peninsula, which has a very short growing season. Fishing offered a more attractive choice than agriculture, but the government made no effort to help the Chippewas and Ottawas get ahead in the fishery. With assistance denied by excessively narrow policies, no Chippewa or Ottawa had joined the ranks of the big-boat fishermen in northern Lakes Michigan and Huron by 1870. Most Indians survived as poor rowboat fisherman.

As early as 1860, in Mackinac County, Michigan, a longtime center of the fishing industry, great inequality existed among local fishermen. According to census data, newcomers of English and Irish stock dominated the fishery and filled the upper economic strata, while full-blood and mixed-blood Indians struggled at the lower levels of society.[9]

Census taker George T. Wendell, an apparently meticulous recorder and a fisherman by trade, visited the area around the Straits of Mackinac during the summer of 1860. Wendell recorded the name, age, occupation, place of birth, and property holdings of each resident. He also noted the citizens' racial backgrounds. Going beyond his instructions, he indicated whether people were white, full-blood Indian, or mixed-blood Indian, giving us an unusual opportunity to examine the racial and economic characteristics of the fishery.

Wendell counted 190 fishermen among Mackinac County citizens, 59 percent of whom were Indians, mostly mixed-bloods. These Indian fishermen are the ancestors of present-day local fishers, and they bear many of the same names: Paucan, Grondin, Charbonne, Anse, Hamlin, Perrault, LaJoie, St. Andrew, St. Onge, Pond, Martin, Truckey, Cadott, LaDuke, LeVake, Trudeau, Plaunt.

Most Mackinac County fishermen were poor, regardless of their racial or ethnic background: 31 percent owned no property at all, and another 28 percent owned between $1 and $199 worth of property, scarcely enough to allow for a small home, some household utensils, and personal effects. None of these fishermen could have owned adequate fishing gear, which would have cost more than $200, so they must have labored for wages or shares or possibly fished a few gill nets from a rowboat. Indian fishermen were rather worse off than the others: 38 percent of the Indian fishermen owned no property, compared to 13 percent of the non-Indians, and 31 percent of the Indian fishermen owned property valued between $1 and $199, compared to 24 percent of the whites.

The poverty of these fishermen could have been predicted. Given the nature of the reorganized fishery, we would expect to find fishing hands who had no capital. Indians, French-Indians, and poor whites struggled in a fishery dominated by well-to-do businessmen, outsiders who had been drawn to the straits by the chances for economic gain. In Mackinac County, fishermen with less than $250 invested in gear dominated the fishery in 1850, when they took nearly one-half the total catch, but the little man's share plummeted with the arrival of expensive new equipment. Twenty years later, seven recently arrived big-boat fishermen caught 36 percent of the fish, up from 13 percent in 1850.[10] In 1860 eight white fishermen (4 percent of all fishermen) owned 39 percent of the wealth invested in the fishery; they had ample fishing gear and onshore facilities. Some of these "big operators"—from Ohio, New York, England, Ireland, Pennsylvania, and downstate Michigan— brought fishermen with them from outside the area. For example, George Atwood, a thirty-nine-year-old fisherman from England, had three young hands living in his home, two of whom were from Ohio and one from New York. Hugh Daugherty, a Canadian fisherman, had six hands living with him, five from Scotland and one from Canada. William Newton, a fisherman from New York, had three fishermen in his home, all of whom were outsiders.

Atwood, Daugherty, and Newton each owned more than fifteen hundred dollars' worth of property. No Indian fisherman in Mackinac County had that much wealth. It seems likely that these "big" fishermen had come to Mackinac County with their fishing rigs and employees to take advantage of the excellent fishing grounds in the area. Such a conclusion is consistent with other descriptions of the fishery. For example, Hugh M. Smith and Merwin-Marie Snell report that in 1866 fishermen from Sackets Harbor, New York, had taken over the Lake Superior fishery near Whitefish Point and established an extensive operation. They also fished along the north shore of Lake Superior, where they competed with fishermen from Detroit and ports in Lake Erie. These big operators owned complete facilities: nets, buildings, steamers and other gear. They hired others to do the actual labor.[11]

In Schoolcraft County, fishing firms from Chicago and Detroit seized a fishery formerly in the hands of Indians. Nelson Boutin moved his pound-net operation from Lake Michigan to western Lake Superior. Four steamers from Detroit fished out of Marquette, and men from Cleveland moved in on the fishery near L'Anse. By the 1880s, Smith and Snell conclude, outsiders from the lower lakes controlled the commercial fishery in the northern Great Lakes.[12]

Many of the outsiders who moved into the fishery in the upper lakes ran complex operations that required substantial investment and caught thousands of pounds of fish. They reaped large profits from the fishery while longtime local residents gained little. In the mid-1880s, two firms in the Mackinac Straits area employed twenty-seven hands, who fished from three company-owned steamers. In 1885 they shipped 1.6 million pounds of fish, worth about sixty thousand dollars. The companies had twenty-five thousand dollars invested in onshore facilities and fourteen thousand dollars in boats and gear.[13]

These few big operators from the outside owned most of the gear and caught most of the fish, creating a market in which small operators could not compete and leading to stratification in the industry. The great majority of fishermen languished in poverty. Most Indians remained poor, and none seems to have successfully competed in the complex fishery that developed in the second half of the nineteenth century.

By the late nineteenth century, although big-boat fishermen

The Great Lakes Fishery   31

dominated the fish-catching business, wholesalers captured most of the local, northern profits. Wholesalers took control soon after the expansion and commercialization of the fishery. They encouraged a free-access system in which anyone could fish anywhere. It suited their economic interests, and locals were too weak to resist. Profits accrued to a very few wholesalers, but then quickly left the region to bring economic gains to urban retailers. It was much the same pattern that had characterized the fur trade and lumbering. Dealers had capital to invest in equipment and, as the fishery became more complex, the dealers pressed their advantages. By the late nineteenth century, three dealers in Duluth held sway over western Lake Superior, three dealers in Bayfield ran the Apostle Island fishery, one dealer controlled Whitefish Bay, two dealers ran the Mackinac–St. Ignace area. These dealers were outsiders, not locals or Indians.[14]

Steam-driven tugs and railroads helped wholesalers extend their influence. Built to haul logs and lumber, railroads crisscrossed northern Michigan during the latter part of the nineteenth century. Coupled with new techniques of refrigeration, the railroads opened distant markets to fresh fish. Wholesalers could now collect fresh fish from the fishermen to be sold in Chicago, Detroit, and elsewhere. James W. Milner, who noted the increased depletion of fish in 1871, commented: "Wherever the lines of steamers and railroads are extended, fisheries are established at new points."[15]

Fishermen as producers had always been vulnerable to competition, even when they salted and preserved their catch. But as suppliers of readily perishable fresh fish, they fell victim to market pressures. They could not hold their catch off the market, nor could they forgo fishing, since other fishermen would produce the fish anyhow. Because of the seasonal availability of fish, fishermen glutted the market in the spring and fall, driving the price down. New fishing technologies, such as the pound net, increased seasonal oversupply for they efficiently harvested fish only during the runs and were of little use when the fish scattered in the summer. At a time when most producers would have withheld their product in order to force the price up and reduce "oversupply," fishermen could only catch more fish to try to improve their incomes or quit fishing when low prices eliminated profits. Smith and Snell noted these seasonal swings, particularly commenting on the regular drop in trout prices during the fall run. They also pointed out that dealers pushed prices even lower in remote areas where they did not have to bid against other buyers. "During . . . the fall when trout are abundant the price frequently drops so the fishermen receive almost nothing for this species and are frequently obliged to stop fishing until the surplus . . . in the market has been worked off."[16]

But the wholesalers made out. A system had evolved in which the larger share of the wealth went to the middlemen. Meanwhile the fishermen were catching so many fish that knowledgeable experts fretted about overharvest and preserving an adequate spawning stock.

Wholesalers had no interest in the local fishery as such, though they had obvious concerns about the overall well-being of the entire fishery. Wholesalers profited more when fishermen were allowed to range widely than when they were restricted to the local grounds. Since steam-propelled boats could pick up fish over a large area, wholesalers raised their profits by collecting the catches of fishermen who worked grounds far from the local community. Formerly, Smith and Snell noted, "the gill netters . . . fished in the vicinity . . . running their catch . . . [to Duluth] to be sold . . . but with the introduction of steam collecting boats they were enabled to go further from home and in 1884 sometimes fished a hundred miles distant, the steamer going as far as Grand Marais. At present during the fall they fish anywhere within 200 miles of Duluth."[17]

Other fisheries have developed very different property systems that protect local fishermen, retain more profits for them, and help small fishermen earn a reasonable living while fishing safer inshore waters. In New England, lobster fishermen in each port "own" the nearby grounds and determine who may trap lobsters in communal waters. Small and carefully defined in the early days, when fishermen sailed to and from their traps every day, home waters grew when the lobstermen shifted to motor-powered boats. Boundaries blurred between one port's waters and another's, and disputes arose. Still, harvest rights along the coast continued to belong to some harbor group or family, and anyone who set traps without the owner's permission met with reprisals, often serious ones. Newcomers hoping to enter the fishery had to seek approval from the fishermen in the harbor who owned the grounds. A local boy who belonged to a well-respected lobstering family might win grudging approval. According to James M. Acheson, "His chances for [acceptance] . . . are greatly enhanced if he begins fishing from a skiff with a few traps while still in high school and then slowly expands to become a full-time lobsterman. Such a boy virtually inherits a place in his father's gang."[18] An outsider without local ties or lobstering connections often had trouble gaining a place in the fishery. Some men were never accepted.

This home-waters system produced a sense of ownership among lobstermen and generated property rights in the fishery, even though they lacked legal standing. Fishermen knew their grounds intimately and felt a proprietary interest in the waters that they and their kin had sailed and fished for so many years. Closely held rights to set traps around islands in Maine descended patrilineally from one generation to the next. So well recognized that they acquired monetary value, these inherited rights were sometimes rented. Eventually, even rental rights became inheritable and passed among male members of a few old families.

Since rights to home waters could not be legally enforced, fishermen resorted to vigilantism when outsiders encroached on their grounds. Local fishermen first warned trespassers by tying two half hitches around buoy spindles. If the traps were not quickly removed, they were opened and left conspicuously awry. When these warnings failed, the locals smashed outsiders' lobster traps or cut buoys so that the traps were lost forever. These assaults on property forced most "poachers" to withdraw from the disputed waters.

In Newfoundland, unlike Maine, home-waters allocation attained legal recognition. Each January in every fishing port an elected committee conducted a lottery to distribute trap-net sites to local fishermen. Only community residents could enter the lottery and the sites were specific locations, not general areas. Excluded from the initial selections, nonresidents could set trap nets only after July 1 in places that locals had not already taken.

Though excluded from trap-net sites, nonresidents could fish in another community's waters if they complied with local regulations. Each community designated different grounds to different fishing gear, setting aside specific grounds for certain technologies. With many fishermen and few productive fishing grounds, the better areas fell to labor-intensive handlining and jigging, and the less productive grounds were allocated to gillnetting and trawling, technologies that required large grounds and substantial capitalization. Not designed to promote conservation, this system enhanced communal well-being by allowing many poor and underequipped fishermen to earn a living on the more productive grounds.[19]

Early in its history, the Great Lakes commercial fishery showed signs of developing a home-waters system similar to those that grew up in New England and Newfoundland. Fifty years ago in Leland, Michigan, the well-established local fishing firms allocated specific sites to the families engaged in the fishery. Families informally owned the grounds on which they set their nets. But home-waters allocations in upper Michigan seldom went beyond ad hoc arrangements.[20]

Historically, Great Lakes fishermen sometimes used vigilantism against big fishermen from the outside, especially those

The Great Lakes Fishery 35

who brought new kinds of boats and equipment. Smith and Snell report: "About the year 1875, parties from Lake Erie set sixteen to twenty pound nets along the shore between L'Anse and Portage Entry but were compelled by local fishermen to take them up. Some claim that their excessive fishing produced the scarcity of fish which has been felt of late years, but Mr. Earl Egerton . . . states that the intruders were very unsuccessful, catching only a small quantity of fish."[21] Sixty years later, a similar struggle took place in Lake Michigan, according to Jim Legault and Tom Kuchenburg: "Pressure in the fishing community reached the boiling point in 1934. When deep trappers from Lake Huron attempted to enter southerly waters of Lake Michigan, pound netters and gill netters resorted to self-help and drove them out of the area."[22]

Fishermen today continue to use such strategies for allocating common goods, although the conflict now is usually between commercial and recreational fishermen or white men and Indians. Episodes of vigilantism have been frequent in the past several years. During the summer of 1983, unknown assailants ruined trap nets set in Hammond Bay, near Cedarville, in Grand Traverse Bay, and outside Ludington. The situation in Ludington became so heated that the local Coast Guard commander wrote to his superiors indicating that he thought the federal government should intervene to protect the Indian commercial fishermen and their nets. In some respects, this present-day vigilantism expresses racial conflicts over the fishery, but such extralegal conduct has a long history because it works to resolve problems inherent in an open-access fishery. And it should be noted that the nets damaged near Cedarville belonged to well-known white fishermen, not Indians.[23]

Local controls in the Great Lakes fishery seldom developed beyond sporadic vigilantism (the longer-term arrangements in Leland seem exceptional), partly because competition was not serious enough. Ports were remote from one another and the fish abundant. Yet clearly, more factors were involved.

There is too much evidence of conflict between locals and outsiders, little fishermen and big fishermen, to dismiss the notion of competition. Problems derived from a truncated economy contributed greatly. Open access led to incomplete economic development, which prevented well-organized long-term local resistance to outside control.

Most nineteenth-century fishermen were too poor, unsophisticated, and powerless to establish or participate in local institutions. Indeed, they moved around so much that they scarcely made an impression at all. They were mostly young and single: almost three-quarters of the 445 men fishing in Mackinac County in 1850 were between the ages of sixteen and thirty. Not living in families, white fishermen skewed the sex ratio until men outnumbered women by 2,287 to 1,311. And fishermen moved frequently. Between 1860 and 1870, 70 percent of the fishermen in Mackinac County either left the region or died. Mobility seems built into the occupation, since only small variations in rates of movement by age and social group can be found. Indians were slightly less inclined to move than whites.[24]

Most fishermen came from outside the region. In 1850 only 24.5 percent of northern Michigan fishermen had been born in the state, roughly equal to those born in Ohio and New York (24 percent). Canadians made up 33 percent of the fishermen. Many of these men from Canada were French, French-Indian, or Indian and may have had friends and relatives in the area, but clearly the majority of the fishermen were newcomers to the region who did not stay long.

Such mobility and lack of local connections prevented the establishment of communal solidarity. Upper Michigan communities were so ill formed as to be overwhelmed. Elsewhere in America during the 1850s and 1860s, men moved as frequently as they did in upper Michigan—outmigration rates of 70 percent are not unusual—but other regions had stable populations of long-resident families that held society together. This group was significantly absent in upper Michigan. Well-to-do lumbermen, government officials, and fishermen seldom stayed long enough to affect institutional arrangements. The settlements that developed were simply agglomerations of people, not communities. In 1860 St. Ignace, Michigan, had no middle class at all but counted sixty-seven fishermen, about two-thirds of the local work force.

The fishery in the upper Great Lakes developed during a period when local settlements had so little force that they could not develop strong institutions. The wholesalers and big operators who dominated the fishery had little reason to promote home-waters restrictions. So free access and open competition characterized the Great Lakes fishery to a greater extent than may other important fisheries of the world. Ad hoc vigilantism took the place of well-established property rights in local waters, and conflicts over common goods have cursed the Great Lakes fishery every since. The fishery that grew up in the region hindered local development and fostered inequality and poverty. Indians, at the bottom of this social order, became the biggest losers.

CHAPTER THREE

Social Structure and the Forests

Lumbering and market hunting developed in much the same way as commercial fishing. The economies that grew up around these activities produced social arrangements that inhibited local autonomy and facilitated external control.

Between 1840 and 1900, lumbermen cut down nearly all the virgin timber in Michigan. Engaged in a complex and highly competitive business, lumbermen watched the market closely so they could adjust to price swings. They could not survive without efficient cutting and sawing practices and well-timed sales. Many went broke. Big operators sometimes tried to influence prices by withholding lumber from the market, but few had enough capital to forgo sales. "Lumber barons" are as much a matter of legend as reality. In the short run, during a single season, most decided how much timber to harvest according to their estimate of the near-term market and their financial situation (amount of capital, need for profit, payout to investors, level of indebtedness, and so forth). Trees were cut in the fall and winter, and lumbermen had to guess about prices during the next spring and summer, calculate their own needs, and then decide how many trees to take down.[1]

Pressed by fierce competition and thin profit margins, lumbermen used the land, the streams, and the lakes as dumping grounds. They left millions of stumps and tons of debris, smothering the land and creating extraordinary fire hazards. They pushed sawdust and other wastes into lakes and streams, killing fish and ruining spawning grounds. They cut

Social Structure and the Forests 39

trees along riverbanks; so the sun heated the once shady waters and drove out the cold-water fish. Lumbermen floated logs on spring floods, gouging stream bottoms, channelizing them, and destroying fish habitats.

Over the longer term, most lumbermen assumed that they would cut every tree that could be profitably harvested. Timberland was cheap and the forests so extensive that conservation did not seem an issue. Market conditions and technology determined which trees to cut. At first, in the 1840s and 1850s, only those near streams could be brought to the sawmills, but with the introduction of narrow-gauge railroads in the 1870s, almost any pine or hardwood tree eight inches or more in diameter could be cut and sold at a profit. The railroad made it possible for lumbermen to cut down and sell just about every tree in northern Michigan.[2]

By 1900 Michigan forests were decimated, and lumbermen abandoned their holdings, letting the property slide into tax delinquency while they moved to cut more profitable forests. Local boosters, railroad executives, and land speculators encouraged farming on the cutover land, often building model farms to show that the sandy pinelands were suitable for agriculture. But few farmers could make a go of it; most quickly abandoned their property. The boosters blamed repeated failures on the farmers' inexperience and "bad habits," but the land and climate were more at fault. Ironically, the United States government had tried unsuccessfully to force Michigan Indians to farm many of these same areas after the Treaty of 1836. Unsuited to agriculture, the abandoned lands lay worthless and idle, becoming public property when no one paid the taxes on them.[3]

Abused as private property, these cutover acres eventually regained their productivity as part of the public domain. The Michigan Department of Conservation (predecessor to the Department of Natural Resources) reforested them, and the lands flourished as state forests, game refuges, public hunting grounds, and parks. With the rise of tourism and outdoor recreation in the 1950s, these once worthless and abandoned properties gained value as places for people to play. And reforestation had brought the trees to the point where they could be profitably harvested once more.

The picture had been much different in 1929, when two Forest Service experts, William N. Sparhawk and Warren D. Brush, reported on the effects of forest destruction in northern Michigan. Their report describes the origins of regional poverty and contains recommendations designed to foster prosperity in upper Michigan. Sparhawk and Brush believed that lumbermen had used the forests to gain an "immediate maximum return," just as traders had once wiped out the furbearers without regard to preserving the resource or concern for lasting prosperity in the region. The foresters opposed neither trapping nor lumbering as long as the land and the region remained productive and the people prosperous. "The destruction of a large part of the forests of a region may not be an economic evil, if the land is needed and can be utilized without any considerable delay for producing other materials of equal or greater value than could be produced by forestry."[4] But after seeing what lumbering had done to northern Michigan during the late nineteenth century, Sparhawk and Brush worried that waste and greed had condemned the region to generations of poverty, although they held out the possibility of restoring the forests and creating long-lived prosperity in the area.

Fires had swept through millions of acres of timberland in Michigan, destroying lumber that might have been put to productive use. Started by settlers to clear their land, fires spread into the dry logging slash, where they smoldered unattended. Every summer hundreds of small fires blazed in the lumber region. "Practically every acre of northern Michigan . . . burned over repeatedly" between 1870 and 1930, said Sparkhawk and Brush. During dry periods, winds sometimes whipped small fires into great conflagrations. In 1871 millions of acres burned as fires roared through the forests and into the

Social Structure and the Forests

towns of Holland and Manistee. Similar wildfires blazed up in 1881, 1894, 1908, 1911, 1919, and 1923. A report on Michigan forest fires estimated that "the uplands burn over on the average every 6 to 10 years and that more than half of the sand plains have . . . burned at least four times since they were cut-over."[5]

Sparhawk and Brush contend that fire and waste claimed 108 billion board feet of saw timber in Michigan, or about 31 percent of the original stand. In the Au Sable River area alone, 20 billion board feet of pine burned, while loggers cut only 14 billion.

Repeated fires prevented natural reforestation. Pine seedlings appeared shortly after lumbering ceased, but fires killed them. In time, no mature seed trees remained, and natural reseeding of pine became impossible. A wasteland replaced the formerly productive forests. A few scrubby trees, poplars, and other quick-growing softwoods, stood on land that had once nourished white pines.

By 1929 lumbermen had cut over 33 million acres and claimed lumber worth about 2.5 billion dollars. These billions of dollars little benefited northern Michigan and its longtime residents. They were siphoned off to the betterment of other places and people. In Manistee County, George Blackburn and Sherman L. Richards report, "lumbermen and mill-owners . . . bought food and other supplies directly from mercantile interests outside" the region. Several Manistee lumbermen who came from Wisconsin bought their materials there. George W. Hotchkiss, who in 1898 wrote a classic history of lumbering in the Midwest, notes that in Manistee "supplies were of necessity brought from across the lake in vessels and landed by means of . . . small boat[s]." Delos L. Filer, who owned one of the larger operations in Manistee, manufactured his sawmill machinery in Milwaukee. When lumbermen went elsewhere to purchase or make equipment—saws, axes, peaveys, and such—they stimulated manufacturing in other areas and provided work and income for people there. They created opportunities for the rise of a middle class, but not in upper Michigan.[6]

Most of the money made cutting Michigan trees probably ended up in Chicago, where much of the lumber was shipped. Many lumbermen had lumberyards in Chicago, some manufactured wood products there. Processing the wood and reselling it generated new profits, which fell to Chicago manufacturers and merchants. We cannot be sure who ultimately derived these second and third profits, but we can be certain they quickly leaked out of upper Michigan and that the loss of money and absence of a local middle class contributed to the long-term problems of the region.

Thomas Wilce, born in Bocastle, Cornwall, England in 1819, might serve as an illustration. Wilce worked as a carpenter and builder in England and Canada before establishing himself in Chicago in 1848, where economic growth offered boundless opportunities that Wilce quickly seized. Within a few years, Wilce moved beyond the construction business into other wood-related enterprises. By the 1880s he owned several drying kilns, a lumberyard, a planing mill for making hardwood flooring, and a plant for manufacturing window sashes, doors, and blinds.

In 1886 Wilce sent his son Daniel to Empire, Michigan, in Leelanau County to build a sawmill to provide hardwood timber for the flooring mill. Daniel constructed one mill, bought a second, and within a few years was producing about 20 million board feet per year. Carried from Empire down the lake in the company's steam barge, Leelanau County hardwood boards were planed and bored in Chicago and shipped all over the world for flooring.

Paying wages to about six hundred men at its Empire mills, Wilce and Company put large amounts of money into the local economy. But most of the benefits from Leelanau County hardwood accrued to people in Chicago and elsewhere. This economy based on the extraction of raw materials prevented the development of a middle class in Empire and similar

Social Structure and the Forests 43

settlements. And without a middle class, the settlements could scarcely evolve into stable communities with established social institutions.

Larger lumber towns developed more complex economies, with trades, banks, and a variety of stores. Farmers sometimes located nearby to raise food for the men and horses that worked in the woods. Such economies made it possible for money to circulate within the community for a while before it left the region, but not for long.

Hannah-Lay Company lumbered in the Traverse City area for thirty-eight years between 1851 and 1889. Operating sawmills on the Boardman River and Long Lake near present-day Interlochen, the company cut about a billion board feet of timber. Hannah-Lay shipped some of the lumber to its yards in Chicago immediately after sawing it. But the company also planed wood and produced maple flooring in Traverse City, where it operated planing and shingle mills and a wood kiln. As Traverse City grew, the company expanded its store into a large mercantile operation, organized a bank, ran a flour mill, and sponsored improvements in the water and electric systems. In 1871 Hannah-Lay began transporting tourists to summer vacation spots in upper Michigan.

This unusual situation, which created a complex economy and kept money in upper Michigan longer than was typically the case, probably resulted from Perry Hannah's affection for the region. Whatever the reason, it fostered the long-term health of Traverse City.

Unlike Traverse City, most lumber towns depended on continuing supplies of timber. When the trees were gone, there was little reason for the settlement to continue. In 1890 the lumber towns of Au Sable and Oscoda flourished. Several large sawmills cut the pine logs that were floated down the Au Sable River from lumber camps in the interior. Together, the two towns had 8,346 residents, and during the busy seasons, several thousand transients expanded the work force. When the timber supply declined after 1890, the population of the two towns fell to about 3,000. A few years later, the Au Sable watershed was virtually uninhabited, and the number of town residents had fallen to 1,512. A fire destroyed most of the two towns in 1911, and by 1920 Oscoda had given up its legal existence.

Lumbering followed a boom-bust cycle wherever it took place. Economic activity and population expanded rapidly at first, leading to the development of towns, businesses, and farms. But since all depended on the timber industry for their livelihood, the settlements thrived only as long as the timber held out. They never developed into full-fledged communities and commonly disappeared thirty years or so after their founding.

During the boom years, lumbering settlements sometimes included several thousand people, mostly young men. In 1860 while several companies lumbered in Manistee County, Michigan, the area contained 610 men and only 362 women. Nearly 40 percent of the people were men between fifteen and thirty-four years of age, most of whom appear to have been single. Irish, German, and Canadian immigrants populated the settlements and camps, along with men from other parts of the Midwest and New England. Only about one-quarter of the people living in Manistee County were Michigan-born and most of them must have been from downstate.[7]

Few lumberjacks made their homes in upper Michigan, according to Sparhawk and Brush:

Most of them came north in the winter to earn cash wages . . . [and then] at the end of the season . . . took south to live on . . . farms in southern Michigan, Ohio, or Indiana. The greater part of the supplies and equipment consumed in exploiting the forests was produced by farms and factories in other regions. Few of the fortunes gained from lumbering were utilized for the benefit of the . . . region. . . . For the most part, they were invested in other businesses, or reinvested in stripping the timber from other states. . . . Northern Michigan has been impoverished for the benefit of other parts of the country.[8]

Social Structure and the Forests 45

Rootless lumberjacks moved frequently, typically remaining in one place only a short time, without forming attachments. Many floated with the seasons. Working through the winter, they left in the spring. Men came to work in the lumber camps and sawmill towns but not to settle or join in community affairs. Actually, few communal institutions—schools, stores, banks, or voluntary organizations—could be found. Devoted primarily to one economic activity, lumber towns generated few opportunities outside wood-related jobs. A few stores, boardinghouses, hotels, saloons, and bawdy houses appeared, but little else. Manistee County had no middle class to speak of in 1860: six teachers, two doctors, two clergymen, one lawyer, two merchants, three hotel operators, five boardinghouse keepers, and two saloon keepers—a total of seventeen. Lumberman Joseph Stronach owned a hotel-store, a common practice among big operators. Henry Sage, whose company cut millions of pines in the Saginaw Bay area, owned stores, hotels, a barrackslike tenement, and even a company farm.

These settlements, which appeared suddenly in the wilderness when lumbering first took hold, were not communities at all in the usual sense of the term. They lacked ongoing institutions: churches, schools and family attachments. Their residents had no local roots and no long-term interest in maintaining the well-being of the community or the region. Men came to exploit the resources and moved after the resources were used up.

Sparhawk and Brush thought that northern Michigan's future lay in reforestation and a restructuring of the regional economy. The two foresters designed a plan that would keep the economic benefits of lumbering and woodworking within the region, rather than allow them to escape as quickly as they had in the past (and often do today). Noting the need for careful planning, the foresters recommended a statewide commission to define a strategy for reforestation designed to ensure long-term productivity, maximize employment, and encourage communal stability. They pointed to the need for regional networks to promote cooperative marketing, efficient transportation, and low-cost access to markets.

Sparhawk and Brush believed that state and local governments had to seize the initiative if northern Michigan were ever to prosper. The state would have to provide most of the capital. Though a good return on investment seemed certain, most private moneylenders would not wait twenty-five or thirty years before getting some payback. The state should promptly acquire as much of the sandy pineland as possible and begin planting seedlings. State-owned local nurseries could provide young trees and offer employment and income in towns throughout the northern part of the state. Nurseries and reforestation promised steady work for a number of men.

The two foresters suggested creation of communally owned forests, a fascinating proposal designed to retain profits within local communities. Locally owned public forests could provide places for recreation and, properly located, protect the watershed. But more important, they could produce raw materials for local woodworking industries. In lumbering days, the trees had been cut, sawn into lumber, and shipped away. Most of the profits fell to people outside the region. But now Sparhawk and Brush proposed that these subsidiary profits be kept at home. As manufacturers of finished wood products, northern Michigan communities would be better off, for jobs and money would remain within the region.

Sparhawk and Brush identified many of upper Michigan's economic woes and devised ways to resolve them. They specifically rejected tourism as a cure-all for the region's plight. "Recreational development and the production of game and fish are of great importance from both an economic and a social standpoint, but they are not enough."[9] The foresters could not have fully anticipated the degree to which tourism would merely hide the poverty of old-time residents, rather than ameliorate it; yet they showed remarkable foresight in their support for a decentralized economy based upon profit

Social Structure and the Forests

retention through local manufacture of systematically managed renewable resources.

In 1929 Sparhawk and Brush had endorsed restoration and productive use of the north country. Their strategies would have helped revitalize the region in support of the local citizens. Already, however, other pressures were working to control resources for the benefit of well-to-do nonresidents, and in time, state politicians chose tourism as a cure-all for the woes of upper Michigan, although this decision little helped local residents.

Upper-class sportsmen took control of the woods and animals by establishing private game preserves and lobbying for sport-hunting laws. First established in the late nineteenth century, hunting clubs owned large tracts all over upper Michigan. In 1940 they controlled approximately 15 percent of the land in Alpena, Roscommon, Antrim, and Ogemaw counties, roughly 126,160 acres.[10]

Wanting high-quality wilderness hunting experiences in association with their own kind, sportsmen established these exclusive clubs and private game preserves all over the United States. The Adirondack League Club reportedly held 200,000 acres in upstate New York. In 1894 thirty-two private clubs monopolized 824,000 acres within the Adirondack State Park for the exclusive benefit of their members. But popularity quickly cursed the New York woods. Already in the 1870s, one sportsmen's magazine asserted, "a man cannot bathe in a mountain lake without cutting his feet . . . on some broken whiskey bottle."[11]

President Theodore Roosevelt scorned hunting in these private reserves as unmanly and a "dismal parody" of the real thing. Author Henry Chase thought the European-style reserves had no place in the United States, where they would stir up class hatred. But exclusive private hunting preserves remained popular well into the twentieth century, when they usually succumbed to rising land values and increased taxes.

Sportsmen set themselves apart from the local residents,

most of whom had little time or money for leisure pursuits. They fashioned an elite style. Influenced by the aura of the English sporting gentlemen, sportsmen established an upper-class code for themselves, described by James A. Tober: "The true sportsman, to retain his identity, must proceed in a highly stylized manner. He acquired a specialized vocabulary, a deep interest in natural history, a code of ethics, and fashionable clothes."[12] At a time when most men did manual labor, sportsmen were to wear gloves to protect their "white and smooth hands." Nothing "looks more *outré*, if not vulgar, than a coarse, scratched and scarred hand."[13] Wellbred sportsmen should hunt for pleasure only. Meat hunters were contemptible, and sportsmen looked down on commercial hunters, who earned their living by killing animals and selling their meat. These, according to the sportsmen, were bloodthirsty butchers, greedy men without principle.

The upper-class disdain for lower social strata is clear in such descriptions, and it was joined to xenophobic fears of newer immigrants, who had no respect for wildlife or proper life-style. One well-known sportsman-publicist described Italians as "human mongooses" when it came to wildlife.[14]

Conflicts between sportsmen and market hunters intensified and turned ugly in the 1870s when it became apparent that game supplies had dwindled and that commercial hunting threatened the wildlife Americans had once thought limitless. Sometimes these disputes exploded into armed battles. Sportsmen hired guards to keep market hunters away from their favorite Chesapeake Bay bird-shooting grounds. Tough watermen guards "thought little of blowing a hole through a trespasser's boat—or, on occasion, through the trespasser himself."[15]

Sportsmen blamed the market hunters for destruction of game birds and animals, and well they might, though habitat destruction played an important, if little-understood, role. In 1878 commercial hunters slaughtered more than one billion

Social Structure and the Forests   49

passenger pigeons in the vicinity of Petoskey, Michigan, according to one knowledgeable observer. "H.B. Roney described the scene at Petoskey . . . where he found 'a large force of Indians and boys at work, slashing down the timber and seizing the young birds as they fluttered down from the nest. As soon as caught, the heads were jerked off from the tender bodies with the hand and the dead birds were tossed into heaps.'"[16] Killing game in extraordinary numbers, commercial hunters threatened all American wildlife, not just the passenger pigeons, and sportsmen tried to stop them.

Beginning in the 1870s, sportsmen organized state by state in opposition to commercial hunting. The Michigan Sportsmen's Association, founded in 1875, was but one of many groups formed to lobby for legislation to protect wildlife. The Michigan association sought legislation to outlaw hunting during breeding seasons. This restriction would benefit both wildlife and hunters, regardless of whether they hunted for pleasure or profit. But the association also worked to prohibit all market hunting. In 1881 its efforts succeeded. Michigan banned commercial hunting, making it illegal to possess deer or game birds, except for personal consumption, and prohibiting shipment of wildlife out of the state. Sportsmen claimed that anti-market-hunting laws were in the public interest, but that hardly seems the case. Habitat protection and seasonal restrictions served a general purpose, but elimination of commercial hunting merely allocated wildlife from one social group to another. Sportsmen simply made their interest and the public interest appear to be the same, and state regulation of wildlife served that part of the public interest represented by upper-class hunters.[17]

Chippewas and Ottawas lost out when sport hunters gained control over deer and other animals. The Indians had formerly found employment as market hunters—note H.B. Roney's description of the slaughter of passenger pigeons at Petoskey. We do not know how many Indians did such work, nor does there seem to be any way of finding out, but the federal census of population does list the occupation of many Indians as "hunter." When the state reduced bag limits and clamped down on enforcement, the Chippewas and Ottawas also lost wild game as an important source of food, which had always been part of their subsistence.

CHAPTER FOUR
Tourism and Sport Fishing

The advent of poverty among Michigan Chippewas and Ottawas reflected a breakdown of the fishing, hunting, and gathering system during the late nineteenth century and declining success among those Indians who competed in the white man's economy. But the Indians soon adapted in a new combination of traditional use of natural resources and itinerant wage labor. Working at the edges of the white economy, they persisted in autonomous groups until the state decided to foster tourism as a solution to economic depression in northern Michigan. Beginning in the 1960s, the new tourist economy, partly built on a sport fishery, forced Indians to make much less advantageous economic adjustments. The development of the sport fishery provides an excellent opportunity to examine these processes, but first we need to review circumstances in the late nineteenth century.

Indian agent George W. Lee toured upper Michigan in the late 1870s. An honest man who worried about the Indians' well-being, Lee feared that his Native American charges had been cheated out of so much of their land and resources that they lacked adequate opportunities to support themselves. Lee's investigations of fraud and mismanagement confirmed his fears. Lee described the Sault Band: "At the 'Sault' the Old Chief Shaw-wa-no is in very destitute circumstances. . . . He is old, sick and blind: and all his people are very poor, simply sustaining life by fishing, picking berries, and an odd day's work which chance may throw their way."[1]

Written in late summer, normally flush times for the Chippewas, Lee's observation differs from portrayals of seasonal shortages and winter "starving times," which had often appeared in past descriptions of Michigan Indians. Missionaries and travelers frequently mentioned the improvidence of Indians and their lack of planning, but Lee's comments indicate that at least some Chippewas simply could not support themselves, even in good times.

The extent of this fundamental poverty cannot be precisely measured. Economic troubles varied from band to band and region to region. For example, in other reports Lee indicated that some Indians in the Grand Traverse area were doing quite well at this time. Federal census records for upper Michigan, 1850-1880, suggest that most Indians held tiny amounts of property; those in the lower peninsula owned slightly larger amounts of realty and personalty than their upper peninsula counterparts and were probably somewhat better off. Overall, Indians owned much less than non-Indians. Taken by themselves these data do not indicate the nature or extent of Indian poverty, or even confirm its existence, but they are consistent with George Lee's description of destitution among the Sault area Chippewas.[2]

Lee blamed Indian woes on fraud, theft, mismanagement, and ill-advised government policies. He described how whites cheated Indians out of their property and resources, especially timber, until the Chippewas and Ottawas controlled but a tiny fraction of the land they had reserved for themselves.

In the Treaty of 1855, the United States had abandoned the idea of removal and agreed to set aside public lands from which the Chippewas and Ottawas were to select allotments of eighty acres for each family or forty acres for adult males. The federal government was to act as trustee for the selections, which could not be sold for ten years, after which the Indians were to receive a fee-simple title. In the Grand Traverse region a few white men quickly bought up Native American allotments once they became saleable. Within ten years, virtually all the allotments were owned by non-Indians. In the Grand Traverse area, 78 percent of the allotted land was purchased by whites in ordinary warranty sales, many of which were brokered by two Native American middlemen, Francis Blackmun and John Ahgosa. The Indians received less than half as much per acre as did neighboring whites who sold their property ($3.31 as opposed to $6.95 per acre). Chicanery abounded but its extent remains unknown.[3]

White land-grabbing helped undercut Indian agriculture. Despite government policies that imposed farming and regardless of threats from Indian agents, the Chippewas and Ottawas had resisted white agricultural practices. The Native Americans did not want to become settled, yeoman farmers. Nevertheless, some raised foodstuffs, especially those who lived in the lower peninsula. As whites took their land, these Indians lost control of formerly important food sources.

Lumbering expanded in upper Michigan at about the same time Chippewas and Ottawas were being squeezed out and pushed down in fishing and agriculture. The Indians turned to wood-related businesses just as enthusiastically as they had previously joined in commercial fishing. George Lee reported in 1876 that the Indians were "supporting themselves by cutting wood in winter, which they sell at the ports on Lake Michigan. As near as I can estimate, during the present year they have got out and sold . . . about 20,000 cords of wood and 2,000 cords of hemlock-bark, and perhaps 5,000,000 feet of pine logs, worth in the aggregate perhaps $70,000."[4] But whites dominated the lumber business and Indians soon became employees just as they had in the fishing industry. When the lumbermen cut down all the trees and moved on, the economy withered and the Indians resorted to migratory labor, seeking work wherever they could find it.[5]

Work in the woods became scarce. White lumberjacks quickly fled to new forests, but the Indians stayed, ranging far from home now, cutting some railroad ties here, some pulpwood there, cordwood somewhere else. As it became more and more difficult to make money in the woods, many Indian men and women began working as migrants, picking blueberries and cherries, digging potatoes, harvesting sugar beets. Until the 1950s, most Indian people survived through wage work as fishing hands and migratory agricultural laborers. Subsistence hunting, fishing, and gathering added to their meager incomes. For the most part, whites did not consciously exploit Indians. Poverty-ridden Chippewas and Ottawas had very little that whites wanted except cheap labor.

After the demise of lumbering, few men prospered, Indian or white. A small number of fruit growers and market gardeners flourished along Lake Michigan's shore and a handful of Great Lakes fishermen and wholesalers found economic success, but most local residents struggled, their life chances circumscribed by the region's limited opportunities.[6] The area's economic woes continued until the advent of mass tourism in the 1950's when vacationing and leisure brought new chances to make money. For the first time, large numbers of Americans had ample free time, long weekends and vacations, and they had more money than they needed—millions of dollars of discretionary income waiting to be spent. Officials in the Michigan Departments of Commerce and Natural Resources hoped people would spend those millions in the northern part of their state.

And thousands of vacationers have gone north. Every summer, they crowd into upper Michigan; their dollars sustain local economies that could not otherwise prosper. Tourists come from higher social strata than old-time residents. Seasonally resident home-owning tourists, who dominate the lake shores, tend to be affluent businessmen and professionals; many are members of wealthy and powerful families. Short-term vacationers who come for a few days or a week or two are typically from lower strata than seasonal home owners, but they are ordinarily more affluent, economically autonomous, and better educated than the permanent local residents.

Tourism thus allocates the region's natural amenities to affluent groups, especially during the summer when vacationers crowd into the region. One study shows that in 1975 working persons (craftsmen, foremen, operatives, laborers) headed slightly more than one-half the families residing in Emmet and Cheboygan counties year-round. A typical local family had an annual income of about eight thousand dollars, but 30 percent of all families had incomes under six thousand dollars. About one-third of the family heads had not graduated from high school and only 10 percent had college degrees. On the other hand, about two-thirds of the seasonal visitors to Emmet and Cheboygan counties came from families headed by someone who worked as a professional, a manager, or a self-employed businessman. About one-third of the families had incomes over $25,000; one-fifth over $35,000. Median family income was $20,700. One family head in ten did not have a high school degree, but 37 percent had graduated from college.[7]

Many tourists enjoyed their visits enough to forsake their former homes and settle in upper Michigan. Fed up with urban living, drawn to cleaner, less crowded environments, thousands of men and women have migrated to northern Michigan. The population in the region from Frankfort north to Mackinac has increased more rapidly than that of any other area of the state. The population of Charlevoix County rose by 43 percent between 1960 and 1976, that of Emmet County by 33 percent, Leelanau County by 34 percent, Grand Traverse County by 37 percent, and that of Benzie County by 33 percent—this at a time when the state population had increased by only 16 percent. In the twenty years before 1970, when Michigan's industrial economy had boomed, state population expanded by 49 percent, but the number of people in all these northern counties, except Grand Traverse, remained stable.[8]

Newcomers came north in search of better lives, not so much in economic terms as in the overall quality of their experience. For most of them, especially the men, the opportunities for outdoor recreation influenced their decision to relocate. We do not have a clear profile of these new residents, who seem to have been a diverse group. Many are well-to-do retirees, but most appear to be lower middle class except for a few hundred businessmen and professionals who settled in Traverse City, Petoskey, and other regional economic centers.[9]

Tourism created new jobs and altered land use patterns. It opened opportunities in real estate and construction; retail stores; hotels, motels, and resorts; eating and drinking establishments; and facilities that offer recreation and amusement to vacationers. For the most part, the new jobs went to newcomers.

Tourism began to bring development to upper Michigan. Newcomers seized these opportunities as well. They had economic skills and access to capital that most long-resident locals did not. They built inns and ski lodges. They put up condominium resorts, motels, fast-food restaurants, and shopping malls. They speculated in real estate, closing in vacant land, especially along the water fronts. Tourism shattered old economic limits. Newcomers got rich.

Tourism has become big business in northern Michigan. One of its effects has been escalation of land prices, especially along the water, but in the back country too. Waterfront property that sold for twenty-five dollars a shore foot in 1960 had risen to three hundred dollars a shore foot by 1980 and had climbed to more than one thousand dollars in 1989. Affected by overall economic growth—the spin-off from tourism—backcountry property has also increased in price. Between 1959 and 1969 farmland values rose by 141 percent, but land with scenic views or near water or developed areas appreciated much more rapidly.[10]

Rising land prices and economic development brought profits to many landowners, real estate agents, and operators of construction firms, but they devastated agriculture. Property values have appreciated so much that the economic return from traditional agriculture cannot compete with outright sale. And as values have risen, taxes have too, making it so tough for farmers that more than two thousand of them in

Tourism and Sport Fishing

northern Michigan sold out between 1959 and 1969. Land used for agriculture decreased by 289,000 acres. Employment in farming dropped by 75 percent between 1950 and 1970 from 9,872 workers to 2,474. In 1940, 36 percent of the permanent residents worked in agricultural occupations. In 1970, 4.5 percent had such jobs. These changes parallel national trends.[11]

As it undermined agricultural employment, tourism created work in other parts of the economy. The majority of the nonproprietary jobs are seasonal service work. Eating and drinking establishments provide more positions than any other activity. These tourist-related jobs pay poorly, often below minimum wage. Yet despite low pay, intense competition prevails in the job market, for the population has grown faster than the economy. Skilled and educated newcomers contest for jobs, as do summer-vacationing college students. Ill-educated and unskilled old-time residents often cannot compete. Some of them have dropped out of the labor force; most are underemployed, usually going without work in the winter.[12]

Unemployment in upper Michigan remains high throughout the year—well above state and national averages. But north country unemployment follows a seasonal cycle that parallels the ebb and flow of the tourist economy. Available in late spring and summer, job opportunities decline in the fall and disappear in the winter. In January and February, unemployment rates approach 100 percent among construction workers, unskilled laborers and operatives, and service workers (maids, waitresses, busboys). Except for summering college students, people who work in these occupations commonly lack education and skills. Many never finished high school and find it difficult to get year-round jobs. As work disappears in the fall, these men and women must seek unemployment benefits. And when those run out, they go to welfare and food stamps until summer, when jobs reappear.[13]

The annual round of the tourist economy, which offers full employment only in the summer, provides motel operators, builders, and resort owners with cheap seasonal labor. The better educated and more skilled workers who find stable employment and those who profit from tourism—store and motel owners, professionals—complain about the lazy locals who will not work. But in fact, winter offers few chances for steady employment.

So tourism seldom helped long-time residents toward economic security. It merely hid them behind a façade of affluence. Northern Michigan may seem better off than it was thirty years ago, but only because newcomers moved in and pushed the former residents aside. This process, by which tourism reallocated resources, can be clearly seen in the development of the Great Lakes sport fishery.

The state has fostered tourism in many ways, none more successful than the Great Lakes sport fishery. Under the management of the Department of Natural Resources Fisheries Division, the Great Lakes coasts in northern Michigan became one of the better fishing spots in the world.

The Great Lakes fishery lay in ruins in the 1950s. Exploiting an open-access system, commercial fishermen had repeatedly overharvested the lake trout and whitefish, decimating the spawning stock. Then came another environmental disaster. Sea lampreys slipped through the Welland shipway from Lake Ontario into Lake Erie. Shallow and warm, with mud-bottomed streams unsuitable for spawning, Lake Erie was not much to the lampreys' liking. Once across Erie and into Lake Huron, however, the lampreys settled into comfortable surroundings and began to multiply.[14]

Sea lampreys are eel-like parasites that attach themselves to the sides of fishes and suck out life fluids. They hatch in cool, gravel-bottomed streams and then swim out into cold-water depths to live. Typically weighing a half pound or so and about eighteen inches long, an adult lamprey can destroy many fish. Sea lampreys first appeared in the upper Great Lakes in the early 1930s, and soon afterward spawning runs took place in the tributary streams of Lakes Huron and Michigan. Runs became so heavy and the eels seemed so awful that people

Tourism and Sport Fishing 59

stopped swimming in many of these northern rivers. By the 1940s, the lampreys had entered Lake Superior, where they quickly took hold.[15]

Everywhere they went, the lampreys attacked the larger fish. Beginning with the cold water predators—lake trout and burbot—and then turning against whitefish and chubs, the killer eels wiped out the valuable species. The lampreys had destroyed the lake trout in Lakes Michigan and Huron by the early 1950s, and they threatened to kill off the trout in Lake Superior too.

Lampreys upset thousand-year-old prey-predator relationships. Without lake trout and burbot to keep them under control, fish populations surged up and down, exploding, pressing against limits of space and food and then crashing toward extinction. Commercial catches reflected rapid shifts in dominant species, especially different kinds of chubs. Then, as the lampreys continued their assault on the whitefish and chubs, alewives moved in.

New to the upper lakes, alewives probably followed the same Welland Canal route taken by the lampreys. They had been accidentally planted in Lake Ontario in the 1870s, but the small plankton-eating fish did not appear in Lake Huron until the 1930s and were not found in Lake Michigan until 1949. Once established in this by-then-predatorless environment, the alewives took over habitats formerly occupied by a variety of species and completed the disaster begun by the commercial fishermen and the lampreys.[16]

Efficient feeders, prone to the formation of large, dense schools, alewives ate up foods that had previously sustained several other kinds of fish. During their first two years of life, alewives live offshore, in middle depths, where they outeat young smelt, lake herring, and chubs. Adult alewives winter in the warmer deep water, where they starve out the once-abundant kiki chubs. When the adults move to onshore mid-depths in late winter and early spring, they attack the food supply of the bloater chubs, and in the warm shallows, which alewives occupy during late spring and summer, they compete with lake herring and emerald shiners. Adult alewives move back to middepths in the fall where they once more threaten the bloaters before they drop into deep water to wait out the winter.

Too small for the lamprey, too tough for the chubs and herring, the alewives took over and multiplied, driving other species out. But the alewives crowded themselves beyond toleration. Because their thyroid glands had never adjusted to iodineless fresh water, they could not tolerate rapid temperature changes. As they moved shoreward in the late spring, many died. In 1967 billions died in Lake Michigan. Enormous rafts of putrid fish, thirty or forty miles long, floated in the lake. Dead fish clogged the Chicago water supply and plugged the water intakes at U.S. Steel in Gary. On the beaches, great windrows of stinking alewives attracted flies and drove off tourists.

From Chicago to Mackinac the fish rolled in. Most communities used bulldozers and tractors to bury the alewives or loaded them in trucks destined for some landfill. But no one really knew what to do about the alewives. A Washington, D.C., task force recommended an expanded alewife fishery, mile-long skimming nets, and beach fences, but officials in the Michigan Department of Natural Resources boldly suggested that it would be wiser to try to reestablish prey-predator controls.

The federal government had already begun to fight the lampreys, with some success. Mechanical and electrical barriers set up in streams to capture spawning lampreys had caught 750,000 or so of the parasites during the 1950s. Then the discovery of a selective chemical larvicide by United States Fish and Wildlife Service biologists opened the way for a comprehensive attack on the lamprey larvae. Beginning in 1958, state and federal conservation officers spread the lampricide TFM in tributary streams, killing immature lampreys before their parasitic phase. Several hundred chemical ap-

Tourism and Sport Fishing 61

plications reduced lamprey numbers to the point where adult parasites no longer threatened to destroy rehabilitated populations of whitefish, lake trout, and other large game fish.[17] To combat the alewives, the state decided to introduce effective predators. Governor George Romney dumped the first bucketful of five-inch coho salmon fingerlings into the Platte River near Honor, Michigan, in March, 1966. No one knew for certain how the coho would fare in the Great Lakes but Howard Tanner, then head of the Department of Natural Resources Fish Division, believed they would prosper. That spring, after Romney left, Tanner and his men planted 700,000 young coho salmon in three Lake Michigan tributaries—Bear Creek, the Manistee River, and the Platte River—and in the Big Huron River, which flows into Lake Superior.[18]

The coho are natives of the cold waters of the Pacific Northwest, where they are born in free-flowing, gravel-bottomed streams with high oxygen content. The young coho migrate into the ocean to live for a year or so before they return to spawn and die in the stream where they were born. Although they live for only three years, they grow rapidly and they are adaptable to fresh water. The coho seemed well suited to a fish-management program. Since they couldn't reproduce naturally in Great Lakes creeks and rivers, their numbers could be efficiently managed, and eggs for artificial propagation could be cheaply acquired from females spawning in the streams. The dead fish—well, that problem could be faced later.

Scuba divers spotted them during the summer of 1966—silver salmon terrorizing schools of alewives, gorging themselves as they ripped through the densely packed bait fish. The first salmon showed up in Bear Creek and by mid-September they had begun to gather at the lamprey weir in the Platte. The fingerlings had prospered beyond all expectation. Given another year in the lake feasting on alewives, the thousands of coho expected back to spawn in the fall of 1967 promised Michigan anglers a lot of fishing fun.

The coho program continued in spectacular fashion. More than ten million fingerlings went into Michigan rivers between 1966 and 1970. In 1970 alone, Michigan anglers caught a half million coho, averaging almost ten pounds each. There were so many coho and they ate so much and grew so fast, that some experts began to worry that the salmon would eat themselves out of food if the commercial alewife fishery were not curbed.

Because Coho did not do well in Lake Superior, stocking programs there concentrated on lake trout. Experimental plantings of trout had begun in the late 1950s, and in the 1970s the United States Bureau of Sport fisheries put about three million trout yearlings in the nearshore shallows of Superior every year. The bureau raised several million other trout fingerlings, which Michigan and Wisconsin annually put into Lake Michigan. State and federal agents stocked almost eighty million lake trout between 1958 and 1977.

The stocking program increased trout populations to near prelamprey levels, but the lake trout have not become self-sustaining. Lakers grow slowly and do not mature for six or seven years, giving the lampreys time to kill off many egg-bearing females. Water pollution has sterilized many fish. And hatchery-bred trout have had trouble locating adequate spawning grounds: they return to shallow water release points chosen more for human convenience than as suitable habitats for reproduction. Recently, more fish have been planted on offshore shoals in suitable spawning grounds, but natural reproduction will not occur for several years, if at all.

Coho and lake trout became the mainstays of the new sport fishery in northern Michigan, but many anglers sought out Chinook, steelhead, and brown trout as more prestigious catches. In 1976 Great Lakes fishermen caught 845,000 lake trout, 500,000 steelhead, 748,000 coho, and 742,000 Chinook—a total of nearly three million fish. Several thousand anglers spent an average of ten days each on the lakes and streams in pursuit of trout and salmon. These fishermen love their recreation, and they spend money on it. They buy tackle, boats, and motors. They charter boats, rent rooms in motels, eat in restaurants, shop in stores, and buy a few beers in the local bar at night. Officials in the Michigan Department of Natural Resources have said the sport fishery is worth several hundred million dollars. Anglers place a higher value on their sport. Fishing brings them the pleasure of many hours on the water with their buddies and a chance to pit their skill and experience against hard-fighting salmon and trout.[19]

The efforts to build a tourist fishery fit into the larger complex of changes in which northern Michigan and its resources have come under the sway of vacationing outsiders and those who serve their interests. Old-time residents, white and Indian, frequently lost out. The decision to build a recreational fishery should be seen against the backdrop of these other changes, all of which built a new economy in northern Michigan while reallocating its resources.

State officials justified their decision to create a sport fishery in unabashedly economic terms. Testifying before the United States House of Representatives Committee on Merchant Marine and Fisheries, Howard Tanner, now director of the Department of Natural Resources, stated that the sport fishery brought in vastly more money than a commercial fishery ever could. He suggested that a sport fish caught by an angler was worth about eighty dollars to the economy of the state but the same fish brought only about $1.25 per pound if caught by a commercial netter. Tanner indicated that in his belief the greatest economic good of the greater number of people fell within the definition of conservation.[20]

Judged by Tanner's standards, the Great Lakes sport fishery has achieved astounding success. The fishery unquestionably brings millions of tourist dollars to northern Michigan, but it is doubtful that it generates as much money as Tanner and other DNR officials have estimated. Great Lakes angling attracts people to upper Michigan who would not otherwise visit the area. And it extends the tourist season into the early fall, formerly a dead period, so the financial gains are substantial. Most benefits initially fall to a relatively small group of proprietors; owners of bait and tackle shops, charter boat captains, owners of motels, resorts, party stores, bars, and restaurants. But these proprietors spend fisherman dollars in the local economy so the benefits multiply as they pass through the community. Many businesses in areas such as Benzie County depend upon the Great Lakes fishery for their economic well-being, especially in the fall.

But how much is the Great Lakes sport fishery actually worth? Without doubt millions of dollars, but not the $500,000,000 often claimed by state officials and other defenders of the fishery. The half-billion-dollar figure derives from cost-benefit studies designed to determine whether or not the fishery represents a prudent expenditure of public money. These studies include the value of the fisherman's time as a benefit along with his actual expenditures. They place a dollar value on the time spent fishing and traveling and add it to the other benefits. Thus, if a fisherman normally earns one hundred dollars for eight hours of work, but chooses to spend eight hours angling instead of working, he has tacitly valued eight hours of fishing at one hundred dollars. Anglers put in two million angler days in 1971 so at one hundred dollars per day, these fishermen would value the fishery at $200 million. This $200 million was never spent by anyone. No money changed hands. No one gained or lost. Furthermore, cost-benefit analyses customarily capitalize such values, expanding them even further.[21]

A reasonable strategy in cost-benefit studies, these procedures, which place a dollar value on the participants' time and capitalize the net value of the fishery, greatly inflate its actual worth to the state's economy. When DNR officials claim to have built a $500,000,000 fishery, they are using cost-benefit figures that do not represent the fishery's worth in dollars actually spent. Still, the fishery brings many economic benefits and the DNR has attained the goals it set for itself.[22]

Tourism and Sport Fishing   65

Faced with the tourist-dollar rationale of the DNR, commercial fishermen found it difficult to gain a hearing for their points of view. Prior to this time, commercial fishing had been controlled by long-resident non-Indian families whose members first settled in the region during the nineteenth century and continued to fish through the succeeding generations. Many Indians still worked in the fishery, but mostly as hired hands. Nets, boats, and other gear passed from fathers to sons, along with the skills and knowledge nourished by years on the water. Commercial fishermen had been able to earn a comfortable living until the invasion of the lampreys; some were well off, but most were hard-working "ordinary" men, parochial, uneducated, and unsophisticated but shrewd and remarkably skilled in their trade.

These fiercely independent men had never organized to promote their well-being. They lacked political finesse and had no way to bring their interests before the public. And they lacked money. Many fishermen had sought other work when the fishery declined, and those who still earned their living on the lakes had neither the money nor the know-how necessary to influence the Michigan state legislature. Later, in the mid-1960s, when policies favoring the sport fishermen threatened to drive commercial ventures completely off the lakes, commercial fishermen sued the Department of Natural Resources in an effort to save their businesses. But, by that time, rules favoring sportsmen were firmly in place.[23]

Convinced that commercial netting had to be rigidly controlled if sport fishing was to prosper, the DNR had cut the number of commercial licenses and outlawed nets in many Great Lakes waters. It prohibited commercial fishing for perch, walleye, salmon, and lake trout and began to phase out all gillnetting, arguing that gill nets indiscriminately capture sports fish, especially lake trout. Coupled with lamprey controls and greatly expanded fish planting, these policies led to a marvelously productive sport fishery, while severely limiting commercial netting.

Policies that curbed commercial fishing eliminated wage-paying jobs that Indians had done for generations. Other tourist-enhancing policies had similar effects. Seasonal agricultural labor largely disappeared with the expansion of mechanized planting and harvesting and the general decline of fruit growing and market farming. And the new tourist economy offered little in exchange for these losses. Oriented to personal service, it created work that Indians cannot do with dignity; these jobs—washing dishes, waiting tables, cleaning motel rooms—are demeaning and often stir hostility toward those being served.[24]

Chippewas and Ottawas had begun moving to cities during the 1920s. There they found work in the booming downstate industrial economy. By 1930 about one-quarter of all Michigan Indians lived in urban areas. These migrants circulated between city and country and many returned to their northern homes when jobs disappeared during the Great Depression of the 1930s. Urban migration expanded again when the wartime economy heated up in the 1940s, but the big move to the city took place during the 1950s, when Indian people lost their place in the economy of northern Michigan. By 1960 more than half of Michigan's Native Americans lived in urban areas.[25]

In the past, when the economy had changed, opportunities for Indians, albeit limited ones, had opened. This time, the limits were more severe than before. Watching well-heeled tourists and cleaning rooms in the Ramada Inn that rented for more per day than they were paid per week, Indian women found out how poor they were. Driven out of work in commercial fishing by the sports-dominated Department of Natural Resources, Indian men discovered their helplessness in the face of state power. Many young Indian men and women moved away to find jobs in Grand Rapids, Saginaw, Pontiac, and Detroit. Those who stayed in the north faced a society in which most of them were ill-equipped to survive.

CHAPTER FIVE
Chippewa and Ottawa Treaty Rights

Michigan Indians had long claimed that they had the right to hunt, fish, trap, and gather as they had in the old days and that this right was guaranteed by treaties signed with the United States in the nineteenth century. But Indian people had lacked the sophistication to press their claims. Their rights languished, and the state of Michigan eventually imposed hunting and fishing regulations on Native Americans.

Beginning in the late 1950s, minorities all over America began to assert themselves. Blacks fought to open society to their talents and energies. But Indians wanted more than their "civil rights." They sought recognition of their rights as the residents of this continent before the arrival of white men. Some of these rights were written down in treaties, but many were not, stemming as they did from the sovereignty of Indians before whites arrived.

Led by the National Indian Youth Council and the Survival of American Indian Association, members of the fishing bands from the Pacific Northwest began conducting fish-ins in the early 1960s. These incidents received widespread publicity, and the ensuing court cases attracted national attention. The efforts of Indians in the state of Washington to prove their treaty rights were not lost upon Michigan Indians, who at least had a general knowledge that court cases had sustained the treaty rights of Northwest Coast Indians.[1]

William Jondreau, a Chippewa from L'Anse, first took the treaty fishing rights of Michigan Indians into the courts in

1965. Jondreau must have known some of what was taking place on the West Coast, but he did not talk about it during his trial. Rather, he said that he found it difficult to obey state laws that required him to waste fish by throwing dead lake trout back into the water when he lifted his nets. In any case, he asserted, he was not subject to those state laws, for he was a Chippewa Indian, a member of the L'Anse band, which had the right to fish under article 2 of the Treaty of September 30, 1854. Jondreau won his case in April 1971 in the Michigan Supreme Court, but the implications of his victory were uncertain, since few Chippewa and Ottawa bands had signed the 1854 treaty on which Jondreau had based his case.[2]

Other Chippewa and Ottawa Indians sought to test their treaty rights in the court. An Ottawa Indian from Peshawbestown near Traverse City, Arthur Duhamel, was arrested several times for treaty-right fishing and served a jail sentence after being convicted by District Court Judge Richard L. Benedict. State officers never returned the fishing equipment they confiscated from Duhamel. While fishing, Duhamel was also accosted several times by vigilantes, who smashed his gear and tried to intimidate him. Most Indian fishermen have had similar experiences with vigilante groups who patrolled the beaches.[3]

Lacking money for attorney's fees, Duhamel could not afford a lawyer to press his case beyond the local courts where his treaty rights had gained an unfavorable hearing. While Duhamel's efforts were stymied, Bay Mills Indian Albert "Big Abe" LeBlanc, aided by William James, director of Upper Peninsula Legal Services, won important victories culminating in recognition of Native American treaty rights to fish by the Michigan Supreme Court in December, 1976. The Court found in *People* v. *LeBlanc*, 399 Mich 31, that present-day descendants of historical Chippewa and Ottawa bands still had fishing rights stemming from the Treaty of Washington that their ancestors had signed in 1836. The state could limit these rights only after proving that Indian fishing endangered the resource. The court held that the state's gill-net ban could only be extended to the Chippewas and Ottawas after the state had shown that: (1) Use of gill nets threatened the fish generally; (2) Indian use of gill nets threatened the fish; (3) Banning Indian gillnetting was not discriminatory. The Supreme Court remanded the case to the District Court for a hearing on these issues.[4]

Unsure of their prospects in the state courts—LeBlanc had lost in district court—and aware of the degree to which locally elected district judges were often guided by public opinion, the leaders of Bay Mills Indian community and the Sault Tribe of Chippewa Indians pursued their treaty rights in federal court, too. The Grand Traverse band joined the suit later. The Indians sought help from the Upper Peninsula Legal Services and the Native American Rights Fund, which provided a gifted lead attorney, Bruce R. Greene, who guided the Chippewa and Ottawa case. Acting in accord with their trust responsibilities toward recognized Indian groups, the United States Departments of Justice and the Interior entered the suit on the Indians' behalf in a case which became the *United States v. the State of Michigan*, M26-73CA. Begun in 1973, the case crawled through the courts, eventuated in a lengthy trial, and was not generally settled until 1985, when the various parties to the suit entered into a consent order that allocated the resource. *United States v. Michigan*, the trial, and the negotiations that produced the consent order are discussed in chapters 6, 7, and 8.

The fishery's legal status remained unclear between 1973 and 1985. No one knew for sure what rules defined the fishery or who had the right to make them. Indeed, some important issues remained in dispute as of January, 1990. Between 1973 and 1981, Michigan officials claimed sovereignty over the fishery and predicted a state victory in the United States Supreme Court. They described Chippewa and Ottawa fishermen as greedy anticonservationists whose gill nets were raping the lakes. District judges and local law officers continued to enforce state regulations even as the LeBlanc case unfolded. Meanwhile, the Indians believed themselves to be sovereign and not subject to state fishing laws. They passed their own regulations. Fishing under the tribal rules, Chippewa gillnetters began catching lake trout and whitefish in waters adjacent to Emmet, Charlevoix, and Antrim counties. They often met resistance from local residents and summer home owners who claimed "Indian fishing" was unfair and illegal. Indians were frequently arrested and their equipment confiscated.

John Salan, Emmet County prosecutor, sought to clarify the legal situation in 1975 and again in 1976. Indians from Bay Mills had begun gillnetting in Emmet County waters in May 1974. Fishing pressure increased over the next three years, leading to frequent arrests and several angry confrontations between sport fishermen and Indians. Despite using small boats and a few hundred feet of gill nets each, the Indians were catching many fish. Salan wanted to prosecute them under standards set by the Michigan Appeals Court in *People* v. *LeBlanc*, 55 Mich App 684. Early in 1975, he held hearings in District Court to show that Indian gillnetting threatened the lake trout in Emmet County's offshore waters. Salan offered testimony and evidence gathered by Myrl Keller, a Department of Natural Resources employee who worked in Charlevoix. The court reserved judgement pending the state supreme court's upcoming decision.[5]

In February, 1977, shortly after the Michigan State Supreme Court ruled on *People* v. *LeBlanc*, Salan met with representatives from the DNR and the Attorney General's Office and offered to hold new hearings if the state would promise a vigorous defense against the appeals that would inevitably follow. State officials refused. They told Salan that they had neither the money nor the manpower to handle the appeals and indicated a preference for the United States District Court case then pending in Grand Rapids. One DNR official indicated that he did not believe Salan could demonstrate the criteria set forth in LeBlanc beyond a reasonable doubt. At that point, Salan dismissed all Indian fishing cases in his county, but other local prosecutors did not follow his lead. The legal situation remained confused for the next several years.

State officials often alleged that Indians engaged in unregulated gillnetting. In fact, the tribes have controlled the Great Lakes fishery with rules similar to those enacted by the state, though tribal regulations do permit the use of gill nets and allow tribal fishers to keep an "incidental" catch of lake trout. Nevertheless, the tribes control their fishermen and have made strenuous, if not always successful, efforts to enforce their rules.[6]

Most tribal fishers use gill nets and sixteen-to-twenty-foot rowboats equipped with outboard motors. Together with trailers and four-wheel-drive trucks, this gear allows the fishermen to move easily from place to place, even over long distances. With the aid of the truck, two men can put their boat in the water across most beaches, even where there is no ramp. Three men can launch just about anywhere a road approaches the lake. So tribal fishers have hundreds of points of access to their treaty waters.[7]

Mobility and multiple access points have made tribal regulations difficult to enforce. There are many good fishing grounds, and tribal conservation officers cannot watch them all no matter how hard they try. At first, lack of experience and training contributed to the officers' troubles, but tribal officers are now well trained. The main problem is the enormous area that officers have to patrol (see frontispiece). Even well-trained personnel will not be able to enforce tribal rules throughout the treaty waters unless tribal fishers cooperate.

Many fishermen consistently bend the regulations, ignoring the rules when they think they will not get caught. Such behavior is to be expected, since there is little incentive to obey rules many of which limit a fisherman's income. A game of "cops and robbers" ensues on the beaches. Some tribal fishers set nets after dark, lifting them before daylight so they can get out of closed waters without being caught or so they can bring in an excess percentage of trout. Fishermen sometimes tie their boats to their nets and sleep there to avoid being caught, having previously arranged for an accomplice to meet them before dawn on the beach with a truck. Or they fish with unmarked nets. Or they fish with legal mesh at the ends of their gangs of nets and illegal mesh in the middle—far enough in that conservation officers would be unlikely to lift enough net to find the forbidden mesh.[8]

And some tribal fishermen seek out loopholes. How do conservation officers know where the 45th parallel is when there are no marker buoys? If a gill-netter can keep lake trout up to 40 percent of his catch, can a fisherman who catches a hundred pounds of lake trout and no whitefish keep forty pounds of the trout he has caught (that is, 40 percent of his catch)?

Some fishermen take pride in their ability to violate, as they call it. At the fish dealers' and in the evenings in the bars, they swap stories about close calls they've had, clever tricks they've pulled, times they've fooled conservation officers. These stories are not limited to Indians or to the last few years of fishing under tribal regulation, but extend back to the DNR and the days before treaty-right fishing became an issue. All sorts of fishermen tell these stories—Indian, white, young, old—it doesn't matter. And that's the point. Violating derives from the nature of the Great Lakes fishery and not from youth or age or race or ethnicity. The game played between conservation officers and fishermen will continue until the fishermen have some direct interest in obeying regulations and maintaining the resource.[9]

The mobility of this kind of fishing inevitably provoked territorial conflicts. Some of these clashes were between whites and Indians, usually involving white sport fishermen trying to protect "their" local waters from the Indian gill-netters who invaded and took "their" fish. Many of the white men who testified at the January 1978 congressional hearings

Treaty Rights 73

held in Petoskey expressed a proprietary interest in their home waters and wished to exclude outsiders. Sportsmen from the Little Traverse Bay area who organized to protect "their" fishing, called themselves "Save Our Bay," choosing a title suggestive of a sense of local ownership. Likewise, the Grand Traverse Area Sport Fishing Association asserted an interest in the Grand Traverse Bay area. Everywhere Indian fishermen went, from Frankfort to Harbor Springs, from Les Cheneaux to Detour, they met with opposition from local residents who felt the Indians threatened their fish and economic interests.[10]

As long as Indian-white conflicts raged and while the legal situation seemed in doubt, differences among Indians remained latent. But the potential for disputes over territory—home waters—was great, since members of the Grand Traverse band, Sault tribe, and Bay Mills community tend to live in distinct areas at some distance from one another.

Indian fishermen from Bay Mills had fished out Whitefish Bay during the mid-1970s; so they moved into Lake Michigan and Lake Huron. Indian fishermen from all over the eastern upper peninsula began setting nets in Little Traverse Bay in 1974, 1975, and 1976, catching thousands of pounds of whitefish and lake trout. When their lifts declined, they pressed south into "virgin" waters that hadn't been fished commercially for dozens of years—Rex Beach, East Port, Torch Lake, Elk Rapids, and into Grand Traverse Bay. In May 1979, Indian fishermen from the upper peninsula took tons of fish, mostly lake trout, from Grand Traverse Bay, Good Harbor Bay, and the better fishing spots around the Leelanau Peninsula.[11]

Sport fishermen responded with outrage, vigilantism, and legal action. Arguing that gillnetting by Indians threatened the resource, the Grand Traverse Area Sport Fishing Association brought suit in August 1979 against seven individual Indian fishermen, seeking to enjoin them and the class they represented from fishing with gill nets in Grand Traverse Bay. The association's attorney, Ted Swift, persuaded Circuit Judge

Charles Forster to issue a restraining order forbidding gillnetting in Grand Traverse Bay. Forster granted the request because he believed that "further gill net fishing . . . [was] likely to cause a destruction of . . . the lake trout population" in Grand Traverse Bay.[12]

Two employees of the DNR presented affidavits in support of the Grand Traverse Area Sport Fishing Association on which Judge Forster based his decision. John Scott, chief of the DNR Fisheries Division, reviewed the history of the DNR efforts to build a Great Lakes tourist fishery after the lamprey-alewife debacle. He argued that Indian gillnetting threatened to undo much of what the DNR had achieved. Indians had all but wiped out the lake trout in northern Lake Huron and eastern Lake Superior, he claimed. In Whitefish Bay, for example, test nettings had shown a steep decline in trout stocks. In 1973 an average of 32.3 fish were taken per thousand feet of net, and in 1974, 53.3 were taken, but by 1979 only 1.7 fish were netted. "It took about twenty years to build a spawning stock of lake trout in Whitefish Bay, but between 1974 and 1975, unregulated gill fishing destroyed the fruits of all those efforts." And Indian gillnetting had begun similar destruction in Grand Traverse Bay: "Prior to . . . gill netting, Grand Traverse Bay in Lake Michigan was the very heartland of Michigan's sport fishing industry. [But] as a result of gill netting . . ., the sad historical pattern established in Whitefish Bay and in Northern Lake Huron is well underway in Grand Traverse Bay. During the last two weeks of July, 1979, the Michigan Department of Natural Resources estimated that Defendants caught about 32,000 pounds of lake trout in outer Grand Traverse Bay."[13]

Myrl Keller, Great Lakes Fisheries supervisor from Charlevoix, focused in his affidavit on the situation in Grand Traverse Bay. There, Keller said, "the fishing pressure by . . . gill net fishermen has increased and intensified with the arrival of various tugboats carrying highly mechanized equipment. . . . The operations of many of these gill net fishermen occur at night, by 'in-and-out' type fishing, which makes monitoring difficult." But Keller was sure the Indians were catching thousands of pounds of lake trout, enough to ruin the sport fishing.[14]

Significantly, this situation presented the recurring themes of conflict between commercial and recreational fishers as well as exploitation by outsiders. None of the named defendants in the lawsuit was a local Indian; instead, all were affiliated with the northern tribes and had no permanent ties to the Grand Traverse Bay area. But they created a backlash that affected local Indians, primarily Grand Traverse band members. All of a sudden Indian children in the Suttons Bay and Traverse City schools were being taunted as "gill-netters," even though no one in their families had any connection to tribal fishing on the Great Lakes.[15]

Ottawa and Chippewa Indians from the upper peninsula had caught enormous number of fish. Pictures of their heavily laden boats and trucks regularly appeared in a sportsmen's newspaper published in Charlevoix, and stories about Indian fishing became a regular feature on television and in sportsmen's magazines. A Bay Mills fisherman attracted widespread attention when he showed up in Suttons Bay with his gill-net tug and threatened to catch every fish in Grand Traverse Bay.[16]

Newspapers in Petoskey and Traverse City published many accounts of treaty-right fishing but seldom described the historical or economic setting in which Indian netting made sense. The articles invariably suggested that "Indian fishing" would ruin angling in the Great Lakes. A person who relied on these newspapers for information would have little basis for understanding Ottawa and Chippewa treaty rights and could easily have concluded that Indians were the sole threat to the Great Lakes fishery. Casual readers, glancing at the papers, confronted misleading headlines that fostered mistrust and hinted of impending violence between whites and Indians: "Fishing War Getting Serious" and "Indian Fish Ruling Stirs Dire Forecast" and "Ruling Opens Great Lakes to Gill Net

Use" were some of the headlines in the *Record Eagle*; "280 Pounds of Lakers Left to Rot in Gill Nets Here" and "Indians Ignore Court Rule, Take 4 More Tons of Trout" and "LeBlanc Denies Conspiracy for Control of Great Lakes" ran in the *News Review*.[17]

Though frequently publishing misleading articles, the *News Review* and *Record Eagle* did not print inflammatory stories and apparently lost interest in the fishing controversy after 1977. During 1978 and 1979, while large numbers of Indian fishermen netted in the Grand Traverse region, the *Record Eagle* published very few stories about treaty fishing and included no pictures of fish-filled trucks or gill-net boats. Indeed, over the next few years, the *Record Eagle* attacked the more virulent anti-Indian groups as racist and printed several articles that reflected Indian points of view.

Sportsmen's publications such as *Outdoor Life* and *Michigan Out-of-Doors*, consistently misinformed their readers about treaty-right fishing. Well-known sportswriter Ben East published a typical article in *Outdoor Life*'s spring 1979 guide *Fishing the Midwest*. In a story titled "They're Taking Your Fish," East argued that Indian fishing threatened to deplete fish supplies in the Great Lakes and that if left unchecked, Indian treaty rights would ruin hunting and fishing. East's ideas are worth following in detail, for they characterize the thinking of most sportswriters and closely parallel those in John Scott's affidavit.[18]

According to East, Indians fished "outside the law." The courts had given them the right to "hunt and fish at will," had issued a "hodgepodge of conflicting rulings that . . . [made] sound fishery management impossible," and had granted "superior rights" to the Indians. The courts had created an unregulated fishery in which, wrote East, Indians claimed the right to fish regardless of rules. Scoffing at tribal regulatory efforts, East quoted DNR official John Scott, who said: "The self-imposed Indian 'conservation codes' are based on old regulations which only hastened the collapse of virtually every fish stock in the Great Lakes." He also quoted an unidentified spokesman for the Michigan United Conservation Clubs, who claimed, "The Indians promise self-regulation, but they practice destruction."

East emphasized the seriousness of the Indian threat to the Great Lakes. Indians netted tons of fish without regard for maintaining an adequate spawning stock. They "flooded the markets" in Chicago and New York with trout and drove prices from $1.25 per pound to $.50. Indians caught so many fish that the numbers in the lakes plummeted. To East, the severe reductions in the fish supplies in Whitefish Bay seemed typical of the lakes as a whole. "The DNR had planted more than 400,000 lake trout in the last five years, [but] the Indians caught an estimated 75,000 fish in [just] five months. . . . Test netting and other research reveals that the lake trout population had dropped by 90 percent in the area."

East contended that a damaged fishery would bring great losses to the tourist economy. Sportsmen's license fees of about $3 million sustained a stocking program that planted more than 10 million trout and salmon fingerlings each year. East believed that the $3 million was "money well spent. In 1976 sport fishermen took an estimated 845,000 lake trout from those waters, 500,000 steelhead, 748,000 cohos and 742,000 chinooks. More than 200 charter boats operate out of Michigan ports and . . . [the DNR] estimates that the Great Lakes sport fishery pours a total of $250 million dollars a year into the state's economy." Plagued by a troubled auto industry, Michigan could ill afford the loss of such a lucrative investment.

East saw little possibility for a sportsmen's victory in the courts. In Michigan as in other states, the courts had consistently favored the Indians to the point that some new tactic must be tried. "The Great Lakes may prove to be no more than the tip of the iceberg in the total situation." But East saw possibilities in two bills then before the United States House of Representatives: 9054, which annulled "all Indian treaties in order to wipe out special hunting and fishing rights," and

9950, which restored state regulatory authority over Indians off their reservations. East urged his readers to write their congressmen in support of these bills.

Other sportsmen's magazines echoed East's main themes of economic ruin and ecological disaster. These articles emphasized the "depletion" being caused by Indian fishing. The issue was never framed as one of "allocation." No one acknowledged that sport fishermen were actually catching more fish than treaty fishermen. And these articles derided Indian self-regulation. East had struck most of the main issues. The magazines voiced other complaints too: whites who claimed to be Indians, lack of responsible standards for determining who was and was not an Indian, the injustice and unconstitutionality of unequal rights, and the incompetence of the federal courts.

Given to half-truths and inaccuracies, the magazine articles nevertheless usually maintained a tone of moderation, avoiding emotion-laden prose. In Charlevoix, however, Glen Sheppard often printed inflammatory material on treaty fishing in his *Northwoods Call*. The outspoken Sheppard labeled the *Call* an "admittedly biased" paper but despite his fondness for hyperbole, he was ordinarily a vigilant and well informed advocate of environmentalism, controlled development, and outdoor recreation, especially hunting and fishing. For years, Sheppard protected the region and advanced its interests by informing his readers about important local issues on which they should take political action.

The vinegary publisher frequently taunted men in high places—Governor William Milliken and DNR head Howard Tanner often received rough treatment—but Sheppard reserved his more rousing language for treaty fishing, an issue on which he never gained perspective. Sheppard seemed blind to the possibility that Indian claims had any legitimacy.

Sheppard sometimes played on his readers' jealousy. He pointed out that Indians had made lots of money gillnetting fish that belonged to sportsmen. He quoted one tribal gill-netter who claimed in October 1978 to have cleared fifty thousand dollars since the beginning of the spring run. More often, though, Sheppard worked on the anglers' fears. In April 1979, for example, he wrote an article captioned "Indians Poised to Launch Net Attack," in which he described how Indians were going to descend on Grand Traverse Bay just as soon as the ice broke up. Two weeks later, Sheppard featured two pictures of Indians who had dragged their boat across the ice to set gill nets in Grand Traverse Bay near Atwood. On the front page he printed a picture of an angler with a fine catch of six lake trout but complained that such fishing was now "a thing of the past" since "uncontrolled Indian netting" had reduced supplies of trout. Sheppard reminded his readers that "Indians have [already] started netting in the area . . . this spring."[19]

Sheppard effectively used photographs to portray Indians as an extraordinary threat to the fishery. In August 1979 he printed two pictures: one of a pickup truck with boxes of fish stacked three-deep, and the other of three Indian-operated gill-net tug boats. Captions alongside the pictures suggested that tons of fish were being caught by well-equipped tribal fishermen. On another occasion, Sheppard featured two pictures of "sportsmen watch[ing] the Indians bring in tons of netted trout." Above, a headline warned: "Violence Brewing on the Beaches: Threats to Kill Heat up Indian Conflict."[20]

Sheppard often wrote about the potential for violence and, in one editorial, he let his rage loose in a dark fantasy of murder and revenge. Like many sportsmen, Sheppard blamed federal Judge Noel Fox for giving the fishery to the Indians and thought that Judge Fox should be paid back. In late summer 1978, Sheppard published a fictional description of Judge Fox's murder by sportsmen.[21]

The rage expressed in Sheppard's fantasy bayoneting of Judge Fox led to action as well as words. Anti-Indian vigilantes organized in Petoskey, Charlevoix, and elsewhere. Secretive and loosely structured, the groups harassed Indian fishermen, tried to intimidate them, and often destroyed their equipment. In an interview, Ottawa Indian John Alexander described some of his experiences with vigilantes:

We knew about the treaties. Back in [19]71 we knew we had the right [to fish]. We knew about Jondreau. Indians talked about their treaty rights. Lake Huron was supposed to be closed to us but we fished out there. A lotta times we fished at night, sneak in! We'd sleep in our boat. We'd set our nets right after dark and anchor to 'em. We'd lift before it got light and get outta there. We kept away from sportsmen that way and before that from the DNR. Now I'm going way back before we had the rights. Like down at Petoskey, it worked pretty good. We did all of our fishin' at night there. We fished out front [of St. Ignace] here at night a lot, freezin' out there on the water.

From there on in, we traveled all over, fishing. I like to fish—been around it all my life. I had a lotta relations that was fishermen. My dad was a fisherman for a while. He fished trap nets. I was always around fishermen so I think it got into me a bit. And I like being my own boss. That's probably the main reason [I like to fish]. You got your own hours and you can do what you want more or less. That's a big thing. There isn't much in the money part. You make it and that's about it. You don't get rich or anything.

So we been fishin' all over: Lake Superior, Lake Michigan, Lake Huron. We got hassled lots of times. They'd try to block the road. They'd saw trees so they'd fall across the road. They put big rocks in the middle of the road—put some nails in the road. We had a lotta flat tires. We've had sand in our gas tank. Screwin' with the motor—took the distributor out and threw it away. Just all that kind of hassle. Then out on the lake sometimes they'd try to swamp us.

Around Petoskey and Charlevoix that stuff happens all the time. Unless you find a good spot like Glen Haven, you're going to get hassled. Around Cheboygan and Alpena they mostly get you on the lake—cut your buoys and drag your nets.

I remember one night we were sittin' at the beach there by Petoskey. It was about twelve o'clock at night. We had a boat tied to the trailer, but the trailer was half way in the water. We were waitin' till about two o'clock, and then we were going to lift. Some guy started— they had a rifle up there [on the bluff above us], and they shot it at us. That was probably about the closest time. When they hit the water, it was only about three feet from my legs. It was a pretty good-sized rifle. Then we heard the car take off. They probably weren't trying to hit us but that was a close call anyway. That was when we were fishin' in Little Traverse Bay, which was open to us too.

There's been guys walking up to—like one guy had a shotgun. He had about eighteen guys standin' behind him. Mostly, well, there were just a lotta loudmouths. It still gives you weird feelings—guys with guns. We always had shotguns, which you had to in those days. I didn't ever go hardly no place without a shotgun. Just for that reason, you know, for self-protection.[22]

In April 1979, 150 men gathered in the Charlevoix Rod and Gun Club to see what they could do to halt Indian netting in the waters off their beaches. They organized the Stop Gill Netting Association. In posters and advertisements the association identified itself as "a non-violent group dedicated to stop gill netting," and during the meeting president Bob Hybil said the beach patrolling must stay "within the law." But the group was clearly intent on vigilantism; the SGN would begin with lawful pressure but would, Hybil said, "take a plan of action if it doesn't work."[23]

Association treasurer Dave Juilleret of Charlevoix said he did not condone violence but indicated that SGN must do something "to stop gill net fishing and not wait for the governor's office to intervene. 'Somebody's got to take a stand. The only time [Governor] Milliken moves is when somebody gets ready to kill some Indians.'" Other members were more direct: " 'One way or another, Indians are not going to gill net here,' one man said. 'It's going to take violence,' [shouted] another . . . getting hoots of approval [from the crowd]."[24]

SGN posters featured photographs taken by Myrl Keller, the DNR official who filed an affidavit in Judge Forster's court on behalf of the Grand Traverse Area Sport Fishing Association. Another, anonymous DNR official thought SGN was doing some good, keeping Indians out of local waters. "I think these guys [SGN] have them nervous," he said.[25] Many Indians assumed that SGN and the DNR were in cahoots.[26]

In the spring of 1980, Dwight Lewis, the former head of

Michigan Indian Legal Services, estimated that most whites in the Grand Traverse Bay Area had little interest in the Indians and in fact probably had no idea that Chippewa and Ottawa people lived in the vicinity. But sport fishermen who knew about Indian netters fostered hard feelings among a small but often ferocious minority of whites. Wherever sport fishing flourished, anti-Indian sentiment flamed up, creating a very different political climate along the northwest coast of the lower peninsula from that which existed in the upper peninsula. Without a prosperous and well-organized sport-fishing connection and long a center of hatred for the DNR, the upper peninsula never generated the bitterness toward Indian gillnetters that raged in the Petoskey, Charlevoix, Traverse City, and Leelanau County areas. Treaty-right fishing had very different consequences in the upper and lower peninsulas and, in general, created more problems for Indians who lived near centers of sport fishing than for those who did not.[27]

In 1979 the Traverse City *Record Eagle* branded SGN a "racist" organization and suggested that its members should "cover their bodies with white sheets [and] seek a charter from the Ku Klux Klan." SGN and its successor group, the Grand Traverse Area Sport Fishing Association (GTASFA), denied the accusation. Racism is a hard charge to prove or disprove, but it is likely that spokesmen for the two groups advocated violence against Indian fishermen, and they certainly dealt with Indians as racial stereotypes.[28]

In March 1982 the *Northwoods Call* reported that Bill Hicks, GTASFA public relations director, had urged a group of charter-boat operators to take the law into their own hands, telling them that it was "time to hit the beaches." According to the *Call*, "Hicks explained that sportsmen and the state have exhausted all legal options to halt the netting and violence appears to be the only recourse left."[29] Hicks later denied making such statements and claimed that the *Call* had misquoted him.

Treaty Rights

He said he never advocated violence, but instead said that sports fishermen should go to the beaches and confront netters when they are engaged in illegal activities, such as stringing gill nets across river mouths. He also suggested that sports fishermen take pictures of the netters.

"I am not suggesting that the sports fishermen should go out and deep six an Indian or pound one into the beach," he said. "But when the Indians show a total disregard for even their own rules and display a greedy and irresponsible attitude towards a resource, they should be told in no uncertain terms that they are not welcome in the community.[30]

Later, Hicks wrote in the GTASFA newsletter:

And the bleating goes on in the papers about all the ill treatment the Indians claim they are getting. If they weren't so greedy and lawless, they wouldn't have some of the heat they get. . . . Let's keep the heat on till the irresponsible Indian fishermen agree to be decent citizens and have the rules enforced in State court the same as the rest of us have to do. This business of grabbing hundreds of pounds of lake trout illegally and then getting a $25.00 fine in tribal court . . . generates ill feelings. . . . Hundreds of thousands of dollars have been poured into helping the Indian fishery . . . but these super citizens who love these handouts still don't want to face the music in local courts when they screw up.[31]

DNR officials such as head of law enforcement Frank Opolka and fisheries chief John Scott regularly appeared at GTASFA meetings. District Judge Richard L. Benedict, who heard fishing cases in Leelanau County, sometimes attended, too. Indians in the Traverse City area were understandably dismayed at the cooperation between public officials and an organization that condoned the sort of attitudes express by Bill Hicks.

SGN, GTASFA, and the secretive vigilante groups formed earlier in the mid-1970s were sometimes attributed to "white backlash" against Ottawa and Chippewa initiatives, with the implication that gillnetting had provoked a newborn hostility toward Native Americans. Actually, many whites had scorned Indians for generations and treated them badly. Treaty fishing offered an outlet for old prejudices, heated to a boil by sportsmen's groups. Speaking before the Michigan Civil Rights Commission in June 1983, former state Indian commissioner John Bailey summed up the situation: "We've got children who have suffered; we got old people who have suffered. If the state were to compensate us for our mental anguish, it would go broke."[32]

Sportsmen stirred up such anti-Indian sentiments. They cleverly portrayed treaty-right fishing by Indians as an environmental threat, much as they had called commercial hunters enemies of conservation a hundred years before. Chippewa and Ottawa gill-netters, they contended, would wipe out lake trout stocks if state-administered controls were not restored. The sportsmen's frame of reference dominated discussions of treaty fishing in the news media and in public hearings, in which whites typically described the Indians as greedy antienvironmentalists and Indians denied these allegations. Clearly, sportsmen had forced the Indians on the defensive in a context where the Chippewas and Ottawas would ordinarily look bad no matter what the truth might be.

In fact, treaty-right fishing did not involve conservation as that term is ordinarily understood, since the planted lake trout that the Indians caught did not naturally reproduce. The lake trout fishery was a put-grow-take operation, in other words, a sort of giant fish farm, and the sportsmen's arguments buried the crucial matter of allocation under an avalanche of environmental rhetoric. No one ever publicly discussed allocation—who should get what. No one noted that most of the benefits of the sport fishery went to middle-class white males who did not live in the region or were newcomers to it, and that treaty fishing was a way to reapportion the benefits to allow local

Treaty Rights 85

Native Americans to participate as well. Instead, people's attention was riveted to the conservation issue. Despite a lengthy trial and drawn-out negotiations that might have led to discussions of reform, the fairness of the system remained unexamined.

CHAPTER SIX
Treaty Rights in the Courts

The conflict over treaty right fishing went to trial in United States District Court in 1978, after several years of maneuvering and preparation. The litigants in *United States v. Michigan* had defined two questions for the court to answer, which became the focus of two phases of the trial: phase 1, Did modern descendants of nineteenth-century treaty signatories still have fishing rights? and phase 2, If fishing rights still existed, to how many and what kinds of fish were the Indians entitled? Based on these definitions, phase 1 involved property rights only and had nothing to do with conserving resources or protecting the environment. There were well-defined legal concepts to guide phase 1, but few precedents existed for phase 2. With these definitions of the issues, many important matters never came before the court.

Given the legal precedents surrounding Indian treaty rights a victory for the Indians and the United States (the plaintiffs) seemed likely in Phase 1. Still, the case hardly constituted a simple application of legal principles. The state of Michigan could have mounted a defense that might have succeeded on appeal, but it made little effort to do so. And acting for the plaintiff, attorney Bruce R. Greene planned a brilliant case.[1]

A peculiar legal field, Indian law depends upon historical events. Attorneys argue about present-day matters by presenting different versions of what happened in the past, usually with the help of professional historians and anthropologists who appear as expert witnesses. To win his case, Bruce Greene

Treaty Rights in the Courts

needed to show that the Ottawas and Chippewas had fished extensively for food in their historic past, that fishing had played a crucial role in their traditional subsistence, and that they had retained the right to fish in the treaties signed with the United States in 1820, 1836, and 1855. As the inhabitants of the region prior to the arrival of whites, the Indians had an aboriginal right to fish if they had depended on fish for food. And they retained that right unless it could be shown that they had given it up. Greene had no trouble showing the historical importance of fishing to the Chippewas and Ottawas—attorneys for the state scarcely contested the matter—but it took real skill to prove that the Indians had not given up their aboriginal right.

Greene hired three expert witnesses, ethnohistorian Helen Tanner, anthropologist Charles Cleland, and anthropologist James Clifton, but he built his case primarily around the testimony of Helen Tanner, a respected expert who had spent most of her professional life studying Great Lakes Indians. Associated with the prestigious Newberry Library and a former member of the Michigan Indian Commission, Tanner brought credibility to Greene's case. She was hired shortly after the litigation began in 1973 to research the extent and nature of the historical Indian fishery and to examine the circumstances surrounding treaties signed between the Chippewa and Ottawa bands and the United States. Tanner wrote two excellent histories while preparing to testify. She had studied carefully and performed well on the stand.

Tanner told of legendary accounts describing the Chippewa and Ottawa migrations to the Great Lakes region and testified about the Indians' way of life and annual round. She then meticulously reviewed the "ancient documents" (historical sources) that described Indian fishing. Often reading critical passages from well-known and trustworthy accounts, Tanner showed how the sources—whether English, French or American, whether explorer, trader, missionary, scientist, or politician—told the same story. The Chippewas and Ottawas were fisher-people who relied on fish for most of their protein and for income when a commercial market developed in the nineteenth century. Gregory Taylor, attorney for the state of Michigan, picked at Tanner's testimony, her research strategies, and expertise. But her statements held up.

A few days later, Greene put anthropologist Charles Cleland on the stand to expand upon Tanner's description of Chippewa and Ottawa fishing. A distinguished archaeologist, Cleland testified about artifacts that indicated widespread fishing prior to the arrival of white explorers and missionaries: harpoons and spear heads, fishhooks and net sinkers. Cleland related how in one site near the Mackinac Straits—a summer fishing camp—fish bones constituted 90 percent of the gross number of bones dug up. He estimated that about two-thirds of the meat consumed by the Chippewas and Ottawas came from fish. Physical evidence of this sort, fishing paraphernalia and fish bones, provided powerful support for the argument already elaborated by Tanner.

Cleland discussed historical accounts of Indian fishing that Tanner had not emphasized—those of Joutel, Cadillac, Lahontan, Kinietz, Charlevoix, and Schoolcraft; and he spoke at length about Erhard Rostlund's *Freshwater Fish and Fishing in Native North America.* He then turned to a United States government report on the Great Lakes fishery in 1885, which indicated that Indians had remained active commercial and subsistence fishers. Finally, the professor referred to research in which he had examined the United States census of population for upper Michigan to determine the degree to which Indians continued to fish in the years between 1860 and 1880. On the witness stand, Cleland never precisely described his procedures, and his conclusions seem vague. Apparently Cleland used surnames to determine Indian, French, and Irish ancestry, a dubious strategy, which might have been used to cast doubt on Cleland's nonarcheological testimony and to portray him as more an advocate than a disinterested scholarly expert.

Defense attorney Gregory Taylor objected in vain when Cleland's testimony strayed beyond archaeology. Actually Taylor might better have encouraged Cleland to talk about historical matters, on which he might have betrayed his lack of expertise. Judge Fox dismissed Taylor's objection and chastised the attorney.

Peter Steketee, a Grand Rapids attorney who assisted Taylor, often had Cleland on the run during cross-examination, but each time Steketee let the professor squirm away. A well-trained historian could have shown Steketee how to discredit Cleland's research in census materials so as to make the professor's opinions seem untrustworthy, but the defense failed to employ such a person, probably for lack of resources. So Cleland remained unscathed.

Greene had half his argument in place: Chippewa and Ottawa Indians had relied upon fishing before white men arrived and had continued to fish through treaty times and into the late nineteenth century. Now, Greene needed to show that the Indians had not given up their rights in the Treaties of 1836 and 1855. Relying primarily on Helen Tanner's testimony, Greene pursued two lines of argument: (1) although fish and fishing rights were not specifically named in the treaties, the language of the treaties implied that the tribes had reserved their rights; and (2) since the Indians did not give up their rights, they must have kept them.

After Helen Tanner had described the importance of fishing to the Indians, Greene focused her attention on the Treaties of 1836 and 1855, and began leading her through the treaties article by article. Judge Fox chided Greene for wasting time and urged him to get the important matters before the court. Greene obliged and asked Tanner if by implication, the Indians had reserved their rights. Tanner had plenty of evidence. Article 4 of the 1836 treaty obligated the United States to provide "one hundred barrels of salt, and five hundred fish barrels, annually, for twenty years." Why would Indians want salt and barrels if they did not plan to continue fishing? Article

1 described the lands the Indians had reserved for themselves. Each of these reserved tracts was adjacent to a well-known fishing ground and, in two places where whites had recently usurped fishing access, the bands specifically held onto the grounds in front of the reserves. Testifying later about the location of the reservations, Cleland expertly showed the congruence between archaeological digs that had unearthed fish bones and the tracts reserved in 1836; it was irrefutable evidence.

In article 13 "the Indians stipulate[d] for the right of hunting on the lands [they had sold] . . . , with the other usual privileges of occupancy, until the land is required for settlement." Tanner believed that fishing would certainly have been one of the usual privileges and that the seeming restriction, "until needed for settlement," was no restriction at all but a reassurance to the Indians that these rights would last forever. The region, she said, was so sparsely settled in 1836 that the Indians could not have imagined that the land would ever be settled. And Bruce Greene pointed out that the waters where the fish lived could hardly be settled under any circumstances.

Despite evidence that the Chippewa and Ottawa bands expected to continue fishing in the Great Lakes—that they had retained their collective right to fish—the treaties also contained language that suggested otherwise. In article 3 of the Treaty of 1855 the Indians released and discharged "the United States from all liability on account of former treaty stipulations, it being distinctly understood and agreed that the grants and payments . . . are in lieu and satisfaction of all claims, legal and equitable on the part of said Indians jointly and severally against the United States, for land, money or other thing guaranteed to said tribes or either of them by the stipulations of any former treaty or treaties; excepting, however, the right of fishing and encampment secured to the Chippewas of Sault Ste. Marie by the Treaty of June 16, 1820."[2]. According to the canons of treaty construction, this article was to be interpreted as the Chippewas and Ottawas would have understood it in

Treaty Rights in the Courts 91

1855; Greene therefore asked Helen Tanner why the Indians negotiated a second treaty so soon after signing the first one.

The United States, said Tanner, had never lived up to the Treaty of 1836, and the federal government owed the Indians money and services. The Indians wanted what was due them and entered into the treaty to settle accounts with the United States. The claims, "legal and equitable," arose because the national government had not fulfilled its obligations. They did not include "rights" that grew out of aboriginal subsistence patterns.

Article 5 of the Treaty of 1855 "disbanded . . . the tribal organization of said Ottawa and Chippewa Indians," and for some years afterward both the state and federal governments had behaved as if the Indians had given up their sovereignty. Since fishing rights belonged to the group, dissolution of the group dissolved the rights too, or at least so it might be argued.

Helen Tanner contended that article 5 had no practical effect, since American politicians had created "the tribe" for their convenience, being in need of "tribal" leaders to sign treaties and sell land. Actually among the Chippewa and Ottawa, sovereignty, such as it was, rested in small kin-linked bands. Article 5 merely affirmed the normal state of aboriginal affairs. Possessed of the land, the United States wanted to avoid large and expensive gatherings of Indians and hoped to settle future problems on a band-by-band basis, an arrangement favored by the Indians, who had a variety of local grievances. So article 5 only dissolved a fictional convenience designed by non-Indians and had no bearing on fishing rights.

Greene's case had gone well. He had each piece of his argument in place and the state on the defensive. But trouble loomed ahead. In the 1836 treaty, the Indians had agreed to removal from Michigan. The United States Senate later added clauses to the treaty that denied the Indians a chance to move to Minnesota and restricted their stay in Michigan to no more than five years, unless they obtained permission to stay longer from the United States. Surely if the Indians had agreed to leave the Great Lakes they must have forsaken their fishing rights.

Greene asked Tanner how removal came to be included in the treaty and what removal meant to the Indians. Tanner indicated that the idea of removal appeared twice in the treaty as revised by the Senate. The reservations defined in articles 2 and 3 were limited by the Senate to a "term of five years . . . , and no longer; unless the United States shall grant them permission to remain . . . for a longer period."[3] In article 8 the Indians agreed to send a deputation to "the southwest of the Missouri River, there to select a suitable place for the final settlement of said Indians. . . . When the Indians wish it, the United States will remove them, at their expense [and] provide them a year's subsistence in the country to which they go." The idea of removal had appeared in the treaty that the Indians originally signed, though it was phrased differently.[4]

Tanner emphasized the permissiveness of the removal provision—"when the Indians wish it"—and argued that the Chippewas and Ottawas did not want to move, believed they had no obligation to move, and in fact had Indian agent Henry Schoolcraft's assurance that they would not be required to move. Tanner had strong support for her position, even though there was also solid evidence against it. On July 18, 1836, Henry Schoolcraft wrote a letter transmitting the revised treaty to the United States government. He said that the band leaders had agreed only reluctantly to the revisions. The "chiefs . . . strenuously opposed them" and had only agreed "on a consideration of the practical operation of the provision contained in the Thirteenth Article of the Treaty, which seem to them [to confirm] indefinitely the right to hunt on the lands ceded with the other usual privileges of occupancy."[5]

When the United States got an exploring party together to look for a home in the West, some bands refused and apparently none took the exploration seriously. One Chippewa band replied, "We give you our answer and do not accept your invitation." Members of another upper peninsula band said that they had thought about the matter and made up their mind. "Father: We all say, our Chiefs and our young men, that we will not go with the officer sent by our great father, to visit the country west of the Mississippi; we do not wish to go there; we object to it entirely: This is all we have to say, our Chiefs and young men."[6]

Tanner had made a reasonable argument that removal as it appeared in the Treaty of 1836 did not mean that the Indians had given up their fishing rights. But knowing that removal was the weak point in his case, Bruce Greene used another expert witness, anthropologist James Clifton, who described at length the permissiveness of the 1836 treaty.

Professor Clifton held sway toward the end of the trial, a crucial time if Judge Fox had doubts about his impending decision. Clifton reviewed the many books and articles written about Jacksonian Indian policy, showing an intimate knowledge of the literature and impressive historical skills. Greene then directed the professor's attention to the Indian treaties negotiated in the 1830s and 1840s. Clifton pointed out that the Removal Act of 1830 established important policy objectives but that many of the era's treaties sought to acquire Indian land but not necessarily to remove the occupants. And the Removal Act required Indian consent; it could not be seen solely in terms of the cruel, forced marches that drove the Civilized Tribes out of the South.

Clifton meticulously described several treaties, showing how one treaty differed from another in important details. He pointed out that despite the uniqueness of each document, the treaties could be categorized into three types: land-base reduction, permissive removal, or obligatory removal. The March 28, 1836, treaty between the Chippewa and Ottawa nations and the United States was, said Clifton, primarily a land-base-reduction treaty with a permissive-removal component, affirming in effect the position taken earlier by Helen Tanner. But Clifton thought the five-year restriction on tenure in articles 2 and 3 rather unusual and argued that it resulted from anti-Jackson political maneuvering in the Senate and reflected neither Indian wishes nor Jacksonian policies. Citing article 13, which reserved "the usual privileges of occupancy," Clifton pointed out that the treaty contained several indications that the Indians intended to remain in Michigan.

Neatly supplementing Helen Tanner's interpretation of the 1838 exploring party, Professor Clifton said that the mostly young participants had little standing in their bands. He pointed out that the explorers included no more than four important men who had either signed the Treaty of 1836 or received monies in it. The party had no clout—no way to bind the Indians at home to the agreement they signed. Clifton thought the agreement did not indicate an acceptance of removal by the Chippewa and Ottawa bands. With Clifton's testimony in place, Bruce Greene rested his case.

Greene's seemingly flawless argument actually had several weaknesses: his interpretation of removal, Cleland's tendency to outrun his expertise, and Clifton's elaborate taxonomy of Jacksonian-era treaties. If the defense attorneys hoped to win, they had to go at these issues, but neither Gregory Taylor nor Peter Steketee seemed to see just how to defeat Greene. Steketee had failed to press Cleland, and neither Taylor nor Steketee knew what to do with Clifton, who had apparently overawed attorneys and judge alike.

Taylor could have pointed out that Clifton's testimony about types of Jacksonian treaties was peripheral to the issues at hand. The canons of treaty construction require that treaties be interpreted as the Indians would have understood them, and we may be sure that none of the Chippewa and Ottawa signers of the 1836 treaty realized that they had just endorsed a land-base-reduction treaty with a permissive-removal component. Indeed, as we shall see, many Indians left Michigan, apparently because they thought they would have to move west.

Right or wrong, just or unjust, Bruce Greene simply outwitted Gregory Taylor and Peter Steketee. Taylor opened for the defense with a rambling statement in contrast to Greene's crisp logic. Greene had set out his plan for all to see: the Chippewas and Ottawas had fished in aboriginal times and continued to fish after whites arrived. By implication, the Indians had reserved their rights to fish in the Treaties of 1836 and 1855, but in any case, they had not given up those rights—sold them to the United States or alienated them in any way. So the Chippewas and Ottawas retained those rights which by implication they had reserved and had not signed away. Taylor revealed no similar well-thought-out plan for Judge Fox to consider—perhaps he believed that there was none to make. Regardless, he began his case without focus and fell into immediate trouble.

Taylor suggested that a just decision in the case depended on an accurate understanding of "what did happen historically" and that the 1836 treaty stood at the center of such an understanding. The defense classified the agreement as a removal treaty. "We don't," said Taylor, "classify it as tentative. Our witness will testify that the evidence is overwhelming that the 1836 treaty was a removal treaty and that—"

"But there was no removal," Judge Fox pounced on Taylor.

Taylor must have known that he would hear this argument—perhaps not so soon and not from the judge—but eventually someone for the plaintiff was bound to point out that the Indians never left Michigan. Taylor should have prepared himself but he responded weakly: "Your Honor, that is true. However . . . all the parties [to the Treaty of 1836], including the Indian leaders, understood that removal would take place." Taylor should have cited evidence to support his position, but he did not. His case had begun miserably.[7]

Taylor's key witness, his only legitimate expert, Philip Mason, had to perform well if the defense case was ever to flourish. Primarily an editor and archivist, Mason prepared himself to testify by visiting archives in Washington, D.C., New York City, Cambridge, Massachusetts, and several places in Michigan. He had reviewed thousands of documents, but his training led him to examine them from a non-Indian viewpoint. Because Mason and Taylor had never figured out how to attack Greene's arguments, despite Mason's careful preparation, they floundered and, in the end, completely failed to undo Greene's case.

Taylor should have questioned Greene's interpretation of the 1836 treaty, as he seemed to realize in his opening statement. Taylor and Mason should have taken on Greene's argument that the Indians had reserved their fishing rights by implication and that, in any case, they had not forsaken their rights. And they should have made more of how the Indians perceived the removal clause. If the Indians believed that they had to move, then there was good reason to think that they also knew that they had forsaken their rights to fish. Helen Tanner had emphasized the permissiveness of the removal provision, and James Clifton had echoed her. Philip Mason could only insist that the Treaty of 1836 was a removal treaty because it was patterned after the Removal Act of 1830. Judge Noel Fox found the plaintiff's witnesses more persuasive; he dismissed Mason's argument and defined the Treaty of 1836 as a permissive removal treaty. "Since it was permissive and since removal from the treaty area never took place, the classification of the treaty as a removal treaty has no bearing or relevance to the issues here in question."[8]

But good evidence indicated that many Chippewas and Ottawas knew very well they were to move and were unaware of any permissiveness. Fearing that they would be driven from their Michigan homes and from the woodlands altogether, some Indians used their annuity money to buy land; others, presumably under duress, fled to Canada rather than leave the lakes and woods.[9]

Widespread migration and land purchases indicate fear of coercion, not permissive or voluntary exodus. We do not know how many people fled, but in the authoritative *Handbook of American Indians*, Johanna and Christian Feest contend that "the 1836 Treaty entailed large-scale emigration of Michigan

Indians . . . to Manitoulin Island" in Canada. The Feests do not give figures to explain what they mean by "large-scale emigration"—a thousand people perhaps? Peter Dougherty, a Presbyterian minister in the Grand Traverse area, wrote that several families were leaving each week. Andrew Blackbird, an astute Native American, thought that about half of the Ottawas in Michigan left for Canada. Henry Schoolcraft indicated in 1847 that 263 families had migrated.[10]

If Mason had studied this emigration in detail—how many people left, who they were, whether they had standing, whether many treaty signers left, and so forth—Taylor might have undercut the Greene-Tanner-Clifton argument of permissiveness. And he would have shown Judge Fox to be completely wrong.

Mason and Taylor frequently rambled. Quoting letters and documents, Mason erroneously contended that in the 1830s white settlers were crowding the Indians, putting pressure on the natives to move. Had he looked carefully at actual data on settlement, he would have seen that population had increased only in southern Michigan, leaving treaty signatories largely unaffected, except for a few who lived near the Grand River. Taylor's case unraveled to the point where he lost track of which documents he had submitted into evidence. Greene's associate James Jannetta politely set Taylor right, but it was a humiliating episode without doubt.

Taylor and Mason missed chances they should have seized and also needlessly opened opportunities for Greene. Mason engaged in a long defense of removal as a well-intentioned policy. Justifying this 150-year-old policy served no purpose and was bound to sting Judge Fox.

Even worse, Mason belittled the Indian commercial fishery. "I have not found any evidence of an extensive commercial fishery operated by Indians."[11] Earlier, Mason had stressed how carefully he had prepared himself by reviewing hundreds of documents, among them the papers of the American Fur Company in Sault Ste. Marie. Taylor had criticized Helen

Tanner for failing to examine the records. Now, Greene turned the tactic against Mason. In lengthy questioning Greene showed how Mason had selected evidence that helped the defense while burying data that supported the plaintiff. Greene's interrogation thoroughly discredited Mason.

On the stand for four days, Mason testified for nearly eighteen hours. Greene's close questioning made at least part of that time an ordeal. But the worst of it came at the end. Bruce Greene had finished questioning Mason, and Taylor was ready to move to his second witness:

MR. TAYLOR: Assuming that none of the other Plaintiffs have re-cross, we have no further questions for this witness.
THE COURT: All right.
MR. TAYLOR: The next State's witness will be examined by Mr. Steketee.
THE COURT: I want to ask a few questions here.
MR. TAYLOR: Oh, excuse me.
THE COURT: Have you read the three-volume work of *American Heritage* on the Presidents?
THE WITNESS: No, your Honor, I have not.
THE COURT: So this—would you please read this, so that we can get a background of President Andrew Jackson and his relationship with Indians. He was the president during this period of transition?
THE WITNESS: Yes.
THE COURT: Would you read it aloud?
THE WITNESS: Yes, "Trail of tears. Although the Indian Removal Act of 1830 simply authorized the President to negotiate for land, Andrew Jackson's requests were in fact orders. Resigned to their fate, the Choctaw and Chickasaw began the long journey from the southeast to Arkansas and Oklahoma. But the Creek who had disastrously encountered Jackson in 1813 and 1817, knew better than to believe his promise of guaranteed territory west of the Mississippi. Standing their ground in 1832, they extracted a treaty that said, quote, 'they shall be free to go or stay, as they please.' Four years later, their chiefs in chains and guns at their backs, the Creek joined the exodus. In 1832, the Sauk were driven from their Illinois villages and across the Mississippi, leaving possessions and food stores behind. When

Treaty Rights in the Courts   99

Chief Black Hawk sent his braves to negotiate with the military, their white flags were ignored. After several skirmishes, the desperate leader tried to lead his starving people back home, but they were stopped at the river. That pathetic series of events, known as the Black Hawk War, cost hundreds of Indian lives. In Georgia the peaceful Cherokee sought and won from the Supreme Court a favorable decision, to which neither the State officials nor President Jackson paid any attention. Like the other Indian tribes, the Cherokee embarked on a long journey west, along a trail of tears."

THE COURT: All right. Would you first read page 450 where I have marked in red; and after you read that, turn to page 445 and the other places where I have marked in red.[12]

The judge forced Mason to read at length from several popular histories of the United States—books such as Samuel Eliot Morison's *Oxford History of the American People*. Each of the passages picked by the judge contradicted Mason's statements on the stand. It must have been difficult for Mason, a well-trained scholar, to be forced to read from popular histories that he and other experts would reject in favor of more serious studies, however convincing the novice historian Judge Fox found them. Fox made his disdain for the defense argument clear. He dismissed Mason as not "thoroughly familiar with the culture of the Upper Great Lakes Indians. . . . The limited perspective of [Mason's] experience and his academic discipline, limited as they are to written accounts of the matters in issue here, prevented him from enlightening the court as to the total circumstances of the treaties."[13]

In May 1979 Judge Fox ruled in *United States* v. *Michigan*. It was a major victory for the Indians, who won all they had hoped for and more. In a wide-ranging decision, Judge Fox sought to educate the public as well as to express his legal opinions. He worried lest the people be unaware of the "basic principles underlying our constitutional democracy." The United States courts, he pointed out, must protect constitutional rights against tyrannous majorities. Sportsmen's petitions could not measure right or wrong, no matter how many thousands signed them. Ever-vigilant federal court judges must resist popular pressures and nourish constitutional rights.[14]

The judge reviewed the long and sordid history of Indian-white relations. Quoting a century-old government report, Fox characterized "governmental connections with the Indians . . . [as] a shameful record of broken treaties and unfulfilled promises." Though often speaking noble sentiments, whites continually met Native Americans with ignoble acts and dark deeds, murder and violence. The conflict continued. "Violence against Indians who would exercise their rights is not a ghost in a history book nor a deed which we can ascribe to long dead, anonymous ancestors. The threat of violence today was documented in a recent [August 27, 1978] article by Tom Opre in the Detroit Free Press."[15]

And then Judge Fox turned to his legal opinion. He affirmed the Indians' right to fish in the Great Lakes without regard to Michigan state law. The Chippewa and Ottawa bands had retained an aboriginal right to fish, which they had not given up in the Treaties of 1836 and 1855. According to Judge Fox, time had not eroded these ancient rights: "The Indians have a right to fish today wherever fish are to be found within the area of cession. . . . The right is not a static right today any more than it was during treaty times. The right is not limited as to the species of fish, origin, the purpose of use or the time or manner of taking. It may be exercised utilizing improvements in fishing techniques, methods and gear." In other words, the tribesmen could fish anywhere within their traditional waters for any species they wished, using any available fishing techniques, as long, of course, as they obeyed tribal and federal regulations. Nor could the state control Indian fishing. Judge Fox continued: "Because the right of . . . the tribes to fish . . . is protected by treaties . . . , that right is preserved and protected under the supreme law of the land, . . . is distinct from the rights and privileges held by non-Indians and may not be

Treaty Rights in the Courts　　　　　　　　　　　　101

qualified by any action of the state . . . except as authorized by Congress."[16]

The state appealed the decision, but the United States Supreme Court declined to review Fox's decision. He had shaped a legally correct argument that drew on widely accepted precedents of Indian law. In one important sense, Fox had simply made the right choices, just as any other well-trained jurist would have done. He followed the force of legal precedent, evidence, and logic. But the close parallels between Fox's argument and Bruce Greene's stands as a tribute to Greene's formidable skills, and to the comparatively inadequate presentation by the state's attorney.

Legally appropriate or not, did Fox's decision serve justice? Perhaps, though the meaning of justice remains obscure. I do not want to wander through legal abstractions here but rather to look at practical consequences. Fox curbed state regulatory powers over the fishery and expanded tribal and Federal powers. He postponed troublesome allocation problems, but by affirming Indian treaty rights, he had taken fish away from non-Indians and given them to Indians; which people would lose and which would gain remained for phase 2 to resolve. Fox's decision did not necessarily shift resources from relatively more affluent whites to relatively poorer Indians; a redistribution of wealth was not inevitable. And in fact, with phase 2 complete, it is not clear to what degree a redistribution has occurred. Now a handful of Indian commercial fishermen net most of the fish, just as a few white fishermen grabbed most of them in the past.

Fox's decision did not affect the economic structure of the fishery. Indians could fish commercially now under their own regulations, but the benefits would still flow primarily to non-Indians, most of whom lived outside the region. The fishery had not fundamentally changed since the nineteenth century; middlemen and retailers still received most of the profits.

The Fox decision restored control of a renewable natural

resource to persons who can trace their ancestry to native peoples that lived in the Great Lakes region before the arrival of whites. In the logic of the Fox decision, prior occupancy produces superior rights, but these rights apply only to Indians. Longtime occupancy brought no special advantages to whites, some of whom lost generations-old fishing businesses.

The weak defense in the *United States* v. *Michigan* seems surprising. The governor, attorney general, and other political leaders had repeatedly emphasized the importance of the case, and DNR representatives complained nonstop about the impending ruin of their multimillion dollar sport-fishing industry. Yet, in truth, the state did not mount a serious effort to win, and refused to spend much money on the case—or so it seems. Gregory Taylor handled most of the trial, with some help from Peter Steketee, whereas Bruce Greene had three assistants, each of whom lived among Indians and worked on the case steadily, day by day. Greene hired three superbly trained witnesses, recognized experts on Indian affairs. Taylor employed one expert, primarily an archivist, who knew very little about Indian history or culture. The evidence suggests that the state conceded the case without a serious effort but fails to indicate why. We can only guess about motives.

Despite a poorly argued and badly organized case, Gregory Taylor was plainly not incompetent. When given a chance, he worked skillfully. He was simply outmanned by Greene and his associates and outspent by the plaintiffs. Moreover, the politicians of the state—Governor William Milliken, Attorney General Frank Kelley, and DNR Director Howard Tanner—were more interested in using the issue politically than in winning the case. Speaking against Indian treaty rights, as each consistently did, would win support among the non-Indian majority and well-organized sportsmen's clubs. Good preparation of the case would be invisible to political supporters.

Treaty Rights in the Courts 103

In 1971, immediately after the Michigan Supreme Court upheld William Jondreau's treaty rights to fish in Keweenaw Bay, state officials took a conciliatory position toward treaty-right fishing. Since Jondreau's ancestors had signed a different set of treaties from those signed by most Michigan Indians, the legal precedent seemed to have limited application. At first DNR leaders instructed their law officers not to arrest Indians who claimed treaty rights to fish. Had state officials bargained with Indian leaders at that time, it seems likely that the Indians would have accepted rights limited to their "home waters," but no bargains were struck.[17]

Pressed by sportsmen through Michigan United Conservation Clubs, state officials soon shifted their policy and stubbornly opposed treaty-right fishing, taking an intransigent position from which they never retreated. The DNR portrayed the Indians as destroyers of the environment and natural resources, indiscriminately gillnetting until they had depleted fish stocks. They would soon ruin Michigan's multimillion dollar sport fishery unless the state promptly regained complete control of it.

Begun as a political posture, as rhetoric, the state's description of treaty-right fishing and its consequences eventually generated policy. As politicians, sportsmen, and sportswriters repeated the ideas, they came to believe them, forming an ideology that directed state action in court and out. The ideology shaped Gregory Taylor's case, forcing him to take an "anti-Indian" stance and to put a witness on the stand from the DNR, who foolishly tried to educate the judge on fishing equipment, Indians, and the ecology of the Great Lakes fishery. Taylor put on a "political case," directed to sport fishermen and his superiors and not necessarily designed to win.

Taylor may never have realized the degree to which the situation imprisoned him. But the judge knew. After Judge Fox ruled on behalf of the Indians, the state sought a partial stay of judgment pending appeal. On behalf of the state,

Gregory Taylor presented several new witnesses. Judge Fox denied the stay and summarily dismissed the state's witnesses.

All of the state's witnesses were employees of the Department of Natural Resources who testified under the scrutiny of their peers. Some of them were instrumental in the adoption of the initial ban on gillnetting in the early seventies. All are obviously committed to the implementation of the present policy. Their testimony often *had the ring of a public relations effort*, seasoned by many presentations to community groups and intended to rally public support in order to influence the legislature. It was clear that the state's witnesses were guided by attitudes as much as by evidence. [My emphasis.][18]

Fox made an important point. Whatever the issues in dispute, however well-defined the legal procedures, the litigants brought a variety of agendas into the courtroom that were not immediately linked to the matters at hand: lawyers had careers to look after, politicians had elections to win. Presenting the issues as they did, state officials gained votes even when they lost the case, especially since they could blame what they called Judge Fox's wrongheaded liberalism. So Gregory Taylor had little choice but to present the case as he did—and lose.

Ideology probably also dictated a search for political solutions outside the courts. Given the legal situation, especially the precedents from the state of Washington, the state had only a slim chance of victory. And given the official political stance, there was no room for compromise with the Indians. So the state's legal efforts were minimal—a *pro forma* show to assuage political constituents. Meanwhile, the politicians sought to get back from the Reagan administration what they had just lost in court.

CHAPTER SEVEN

State Efforts to Regain Control

Extralegal efforts to halt treaty-right fishing intensified after Judge Fox's May 1979 ruling. Vigilante activity burst forth sporadically over the next several years, usually flaring up when Indians fished in new waters, but continuing to smolder even in places where they had netted for years. Threats of death and injury continued, but fortunately whites limited themselves to harassment and destruction of property. Local police and prosecutors seldom took action against vigilantes, though they frequently knew the culprit's identity. In at least one case, law officers participated in vigilante activities.[1]

The Michigan United Conservation Clubs organized a petition campaign and a series of "Save-Our-Fish" political rallies designed to attract attention and bring a political end to the dispute. The rallies typically attracted only a few hundred supporters but drew substantial media attention, and the petition campaign claimed sixty thousand signatures.[2]

Sensing the advantages in opposing treaty-right fishing, with public opinion running heavily against it, state politicians tried to reap the benefits of anti-Indian statements. Frank Kelley, the flamboyant attorney general, turned Indian fishing to his advantage, using every opportunity to rail against treaty rights and the federal government. According to Kelley, Michigan had "never discriminated against Indians," and Indians were "not entitled to special rights." Kelley fumed:

The state of Michigan was not a party to the treaties and now . . . 100 years later, we have the federal government and Indians ganging up and blaming us for not giving carte blanche authority to Indians to take anything they want from our own fishery and our own Great Lakes.

I think that's because the federal government lacks . . . the moral courage to take action to upgrade these treaties and treat the Indian fishing business as a modern business and not as a bunch of Indians paddling a canoe in 1835.[3]

Governor William Milliken, too, exploited treaty fishing. He frequently castigated "Indian fishing" and sent well-publicized letters of protest to officials in the Carter administration. Mingling with friendly sport fishermen–protestors who had gathered outside his birthday party fund-raiser in the Park Place Hotel in Traverse City, Milliken said: "I'm putting all the effort I can into this issue. . . . I wish you luck in your efforts and I hope you will wish me luck in mine. . . . What you're doing tonight is one way to make a point." Milliken's wife wished the crowd "Good Luck!" One of the signs carried by the protestors read "Fox is Andrus Gestapo." Other placards variously attacked the Bureau of Indian Affairs, Secretary of the Interior Cecil Andrus, gill nets, and Indians.[4]

Milliken solicited popular favor in this fashion until he left office in January 1983. His message remained constant: Indians were destroying the fishery, and if something were not done soon, white men would turn to violence. Gill nets must be stopped before they ruined the popular (and lucrative) sport-fishing industry.

Was Milliken telling the truth? Were Chippewa and Ottawa fishermen "destroying" the sport fishery? The answer depends on what standards are used, but Milliken had certainly exaggerated the effects of gillnetting. Native Americans did not net in inland lakes, where most sport fishing takes place; they destroyed nothing in these popular fisheries. Nor were they catching Great Lakes salmon. Lake trout were the issue, not sport fishing as a whole.

During the height of the midsummer tourist season the

State Efforts to Regain Control 107

salmon scattered, making it more difficult for sport fishermen to catch them. Instead, lake trout were the primary target of the July-August fishery, and gillnetting did greatly reduce trout populations. Indians caught tons of lakers. State-run tests show that the numbers of trout declined precipitously after concentrated Indian gillnetting. Summer trolling became so poor in some gillnetted areas that sport fishermen quit angling altogether and charter-boat owners moved to ports where no treaty fishing had yet taken place. Indian fishing did not ruin the fishery, as Milliken often claimed, but it did reduce lake trout supplies to the point that it wrecked summer trolling and threatened the livelihood of charter captains.[5]

Milliken's pronouncements on treaty-right fishing brought him favorable publicity. Headlines in the January 28, 1981, Sault Ste. Marie *Evening News* announced: "Milliken Asks Halt to Indian Fishing." The story described how the governor had written newly elected President Ronald Reagan, "asking him to rescind federal fishing rules protecting Indian fishing rights in the Great Lakes. Milliken said former President Carter . . . had been guilty of an 'abuse of power' in letting the Department of the Interior allow virtually unlimited fishing against the wishes of the people of the state of Michigan." The *Evening News* quoted Milliken's letter: "The people of Michigan are being told that the Department of Interior may set aside all federal laws, pre-empt all state laws and threaten the destruction of the fisheries of the Great Lakes because the president [Carter] wants it that way."[6] However popular and politically expedient, statements of this sort provoked conflict and undermined efforts to find an equitable resolution for Indian-white differences.

Other politicians used similar tactics, rejecting the legitimacy of Indian rights to appeal to their constituents. Congressman John Dingell and fourteen other members of the Michigan congressional delegation sponsored an amendment to the federal Black Bass Act that would have outlawed commercial sale of lake trout. Though popular with sport fishermen, Dingell's bill stood little chance of passage and died in committee.[7]

Congressman Robert Davis of northern Michigan told his constituents that he believed "congressional action" was more likely to settle the Indian fishing problem than lawsuits or negotiation. In fall 1979 Davis wrote in the *Evening News* that he felt it imperative to take congressional action to solve Indian fishing difficulties. The issue was too hot to postpone, and he had urged the House committees to take up his bills, which would renew state control over the fishery.[8] Three years later Davis published similar views. Contending that "no person . . . should be exempt from the law because of race," Davis explained that he had introduced bills to "change the treaties, and to give total jurisdiction over the waters to the state." Davis had to admit, however, that his bills had little support in Congress.[9]

Department of Natural Resources officials often spoke intemperately about "Indian fishing." The department supported the interests of sportsmen's groups. At meetings of various groups, DNR staff members criticized the Indians and repeated departmental propaganda against "unregulated" gill-net fishing. Nevertheless, inasmuch as Judge Fox's decision had left allocation issues unsettled, the DNR was forced to meet with the Indian tribes to discuss ways to implement the court ruling. DNR negotiators behaved as if they still controlled the fishery. They insulted the Indians, frequently offering proposals to the Chippewa and Ottawa leaders without prior notice while steadfastly refusing to recognize that the Indians could probably establish ownership to one-half the fish in the ceded waters and that treaty rights superseded state law. By the spring of 1980, after meeting for a few months, tribal negotiators had come to believe that state officials had little commitment to the talks and were bargaining in bad faith.

The Indians had reason to be suspicious, for the state in-

State Efforts to Regain Control   109

vited Thomas Washington of Michigan United Conservation Clubs and Andy Pelt of the Michigan Steelheaders and others who had frequently made inflammatory remarks about treaty fishing to attend negotiations. Moreover, Howard Tanner, head of the DNR, who sometimes represented the state, clearly discounted Indian claims and seemed unable to control his temper. During a May 1980 meeting, Tanner raged: "The tribes have fished themselves into a hole. Today you're running out of fish in the north and into more and more public opposition to your destructive fishing in the south. Your final harvest will be a great public animosity for the tribes, for your federal agencies, for your court system, and for the president you serve."[10] Tanner's emotionalism halted the meeting. Indian leaders walked out after accusing Tanner of fomenting racism and violence.[11]

No doubt Tanner's rage and his comments reflected his personal beliefs more than public policy, but state officials generally behaved as if they had little respect for Indian rights. They betrayed their insincerity when the DNR chief of law enforcement, Frank Opolka, ordered Michigan's wholesale fish buyers not to buy gill-netted fish from Indians if they wanted to "preserve the integrity of their . . . licenses." Opolka was responding to a court-ordered stay that briefly restored state control of the fishery, but he betrayed disdain for the Indians in acting without consulting the tribal leaders or even giving them notice. Attorneys for the Indians had Opolka's directive quashed before it ever took effect.[12]

Negotiators continued to meet during the year and a half between Judge Fox's decision and Ronald Reagan's inauguration in January 1981 without settling anything. Discussions among these longtime antagonists had little chance of success without guidance from the court or the federal government, but neither intervened. Among state officials only John Scott believed that the talks could accommodate Indian and white interests in a settlement. Later, Scott realized that the state might win at the negotiating table what it would surely lose in court. But in 1979 and 1980 state officials simply talked. Nothing got done.[13]

Indian negotiators floundered. Living in Boulder, Colorado, lawyer Bruce Greene had difficulty maintaining contact with the case. In addition, the flamboyance that made him a brilliant courtroom performer served him ill in negotiations. The other Indian attorneys never forced the state to talk seriously, and except for Joseph Lumsden, tribal representatives lacked the skills to seize the initiative from the DNR and establish their political rights. Frequently succumbing to frustration, they never got the talks off dead center.

Delay served state interests, for Ronald Reagan seemed assured of election in 1980, and he had promised to solve Michigan's Indian problem. Yet it seems improbable that state officials consciously delayed the proceedings by engaging in fruitless and time-consuming discussions. Rather, the negotiations reflect an inability of DNR officials to accept the legitimacy of treaty rights after 150 years of Indian subservience to whites.

In fall 1980, late in an election campaign he would certainly win, Ronald Reagan wrote a widely publicized letter to Michigan sportsmen promising that as president he would "recognize and support the traditional precedence of the states to manage fish, wildlife and habitat within their boundaries" and that he believed in state supremacy in water law. The Reagan administration, he promised, would review Department of the Interior fishing regulations and "eliminate those that are unnecessary or which are more properly the province of state and local government."[14]

Reagan's national chairwoman for conservation concerns, Tanya Metaka, told Michigan sportsmen that Reagan's platform recognized "treaty fishing rights on tribal lands," but she noted that Lake Michigan was "not a tribal land." Reagan, she said, "considers the Indian fishing and hunting controversy . . . 'a very touchy problem,'" which the Carter administration had ignored. "The whole tenor of the Reagan philosophy

State Efforts to Regain Control 111

is if there is a problem in Michigan, it is better to have the state decide how to solve it because the state people are closer to the problem. . . . The governor [Reagan] believes he is the candidate for the outdoor sportsmen."[15] It didn't take much reading between the lines to figure out where Reagan stood on Indian fishing rights.

As early as the summer of 1980, one longtime observer of the controversy noted that Indian leaders were showing a new enthusiasm for settlement talks since they would lose negotiating leverage once the Reagan administration took control. Indian denials rang hollow. Clearly, a Reagan victory would undermine their ability to bargain.[16]

Once in power, the Reagan administration moved quickly to fulfill its promises to Michigan sportsmen and politicians. The tribes fished according to rules they had developed with expert advice from the United States Fish and Wildlife Service. First established in 1979, these rules became federal regulations in a "Memorandum of Understanding" between the tribes and Secretary of the Interior Cecil Andrus. The rules established seasonal closures and size limits that closely resembled state regulations for commercial fishermen, but they permitted use of gill nets and allowed fishermen to keep an "incidental" catch of lake trout. The federal regulations "preempted the field" and prevented the state from enforcing its rules on the Indians. Without the federal rules in place, Michigan officials might be able to apply state law to the tribes irrespective of treaty rights. State law would fill the void created by federal absence. The state could apparently regain control over the fishery if Reagan's Department of the Interior would drop its rules.[17]

Throughout the fall of 1980, Michigan Congressman Guy Vander Jagt worked quietly to alter the federal fishing rules. Vander Jagt's district included the "gold coast" tourist region of Michigan, but he had avoided irresponsible publicity seeking for more practical behind-the-scenes maneuvering. Shortly after Reagan's election, Vander Jagt asked the president-elect's transition team not to renew the soon-to-expire Indian fishing regulations. But outgoing Secretary Cecil Andrus extended the rules until May 1981 and temporarily postponed the chance for renewed state control.

Sportsmen had objected to the rules from their inception in November 1979. Attorney for the Grand Traverse Area Sport Fishing Association Ted Swift wrote to Interior Secretary Cecil Andrus in December 1979 claiming that the rules "were purely and simply designed to bolster the efforts of the Indian bands as opposed to the claimed purpose of preventing the further depletion of a great natural resource." The Department of the Interior had neither conducted hearings on the matter nor made a serious effort to assess how the rules would affect Great Lakes fish.

Swift had strong support for his argument. He pointed out that the James Jannetta who had written the rules as attorney-adviser, Office of the Solicitor, Division of Indian affairs, Department of the Interior, was the same James Jannetta who had close personal ties with the Sault band. He had done legal work for the band and had acted as a legal researcher for Bruce Greene in *United States* v. *Michigan*. His wife had been tribal attorney at Bay Mills. It was a gross conflict of interest.[18]

Jannetta, it would seem, had left Michigan courtrooms to advance Indian legal interests in Washington, D.C. But when James Watt took control in January 1981, Jannetta and others with similar views would no longer hold sway.

Congressman Vander Jagt kept pressing the Department of the Interior to let the Memorandum of Understanding expire. In April he reported that he had spoken with Interior Secretary James Watt about Indian fishing and that he and Watt "were thinking along the same lines." Vander Jagt said he felt "very optimistic" that as a result of his conversations with Watt, "the Great Lakes fishery may well be saved." If the rules were to be rescinded or allowed to expire "we feel that Michigan would have a much greater voice in future regulations on the Great Lakes."[19]

State Efforts to Regain Control

Vander Jagt had apparently been the first to see the advantages of this political strategy for limiting the impact of Judge Fox's decision. He and two attorneys for the sport fishermen, Ted Swift and Steve Schultz, now believed that the courtroom promised certain defeat but that political pressure and negotiations could advance state and sport-fishing interests.

Other politicians supported Vander Jagt's initiatives. Governor Milliken had sought help with his Indian troubles from President Reagan, and Democratic Congressman John Dingell had lobbied at Interior, but most Michigan politicians failed to see how to seize the advantages offered by the newly elected regime. At times, Milliken and DNR Director Howard Tanner foolishly castigated the Department of the Interior after James Watt had become secretary.

On April 12 Vander Jagt announced that Secretary Watt had written Governor Milliken and the three tribes informing them that he would not renew Indian fishing rules for the Great Lakes. The congressman "said he had asked Watt to scrap the rules because they [had] not adequately protected the Great Lakes fishery." He hoped that the state would now act to conserve the resource.[20]

Citing a general and serious decline in the Great Lakes fishery, especially lake trout, Secretary Watt wrote that his department would violate its "conservation mission" and its "stewardship of the Nation's natural resources" if it allowed the regulations to continue. He recognized his "responsibility for tribal treaty rights" but said the rules had failed to protect the resource. He invited the disputants to gather in Washinton to develop a "consensus management program." Meanwhile Secretary Watt indicated that he believed the state of Michigan could regulate Indian fishing for conservation purposes in accord with the reasoning in the Michigan Supreme Court decision in *People v. LeBlanc.*[21]

Secretary Watt's decision to discontinue federal fishing rules came under fire from liberal supporters of Indian rights, who contended that it reflected President Reagan's general insensitivity to minority issues. Environmental organizations also criticized Watt's decision, even though it called for standards of resource preservation. In the ideologically charged atmosphere of 1981, liberals and conservationists saw only the red flag of Watt's rhetoric and never seriously considered the practical effects of his actions.

The Indians, anticipating the about-face, had pushed the Department of the Interior to renew the fishing regulations. As early as February 1981 Bruce Greene had sent detailed information to Interior, pointing out that equity and good sense dictated renewal of the rules, which protected the resource while guarding the Indians. In a lengthy confidential statement, Greene bluntly argued that the tribes would view nonrenewal as a "gross dereliction" of the secretary's fiduciary duty as trustee for the tribes. It was without doubt a serious allegation.[22]

Vander Jagt and Watt had opened an interesting opportunity for the state to restore some of its regulatory control over the fishery, but state officials hesitated, uncertain, as they had been a year before, just how to proceed. In May 1980 the United States Sixth Circuit Court of Appeals had stayed Judge Fox's decision pending the outcome of the state's appeal. Michigan could have applied conservation-based restrictions on the fishery at that time. After showing that gillnetting threatened the fishery, or parts of it, the state could have selectively outlawed use of the nets. Grand Traverse Area Sport Fishing Association attorney Ted Swift had successfully used such a strategy to argue for elimination of Indian gillnetting in lower Grand Traverse Bay. He had based his case on the Michigan Supreme Court ruling in *People v. LeBlanc*, in which the court had ruled that the state could control Indian fishing if it was able to show that the Indians threatened the well-being of the resource. Instead of demonstrating that Indian gillnetting threatened the resource, however, the state had simply grabbed control, prohibited use of gill nets, and threatened wholesalers who bought lake trout from Indians. Such short-

State Efforts to Regain Control 115

sighted actions forced the Sixth Circuit to modify its stay and reinstitute the rules defined in the 1979 Memorandum of Understanding. The state had blundered, ruining a marvelous opportunity. Perhaps the actions revealed that conservation was not the matter in dispute.[23]

Remembering the 1980 fiasco, state officials acted with extraordinary timidity in 1981. Instead of seizing the chance Watt and Vander Jagt had created, the state devised a transparent scheme. When the federal rules expired, Governor Milliken declared a state of emergency so the Michigan Natural Resources Commission could set guidelines for Indian fishing. Howard Tanner wrote some lax regulations, which the commission quickly passed. Then the assistant attorney general rushed them to the appeals court in Cincinnati, where he asked the judges to impose the emergency rules on the Indians.

Tanner's new rules allowed gill-net fishing in all the ceded waters, except small areas around Little Traverse and Grand Traverse bays. Sportsmen complained that Tanner's rules threw biology to the winds, as they put it. One commission member reported that Tanner had convinced the commission "that a chance to gain some control over Indian fishing was more important than biology at this point." The Detroit *Free Press* reported that Governor Milliken hoped that the tribes would not object to the lax rules, the appeals court would accept them, and the state would have regained a toehold toward control of the fishery.[24]

These state rules never took effect. Indian attorneys successfully argued that tribal fishing rules were already in place and that federal withdrawal had not left a void. They contended that the state could only resume regulation by showing a threat to the fishery resource, something the state had never seriously tried to do.[25]

Michigan officials had twice bungled opportunities to gain some control over Indian fishing. For years, they had argued that Indians with gill nets threatened the fishery and that gill nets had to be outlawed in the interests of conservation. The appeals court stay in 1980 and Secretary Watt's nonrenewal of the fishing rules were chances to prove that its rhetoric had a basis in fact and that the state should be allowed to manage the fishery in order to protect the resource. Such a case might have succeeded, for test nettings suggested that concentrated Indian gillnetting was decimating stocks of lake trout. Indians could bring in fish biologists to argue that lake trout constituted a put-grow-take fishery because the trout did not naturally reproduce. They could maintain that allocation, not conservation, was the issue. But the state could counter that gillnetting captured the mature trout before they could spawn. In other words, both the state and the Indians had evidence to support their positions.

Beginning with the poorly planned and underfinanced federal district court case, the state's actions between 1978 and the spring of 1981 seem remarkably inept. None of the state leaders offered a reasoned response to Indian fishing. Politicians courted votes without trying to realize mutually beneficial resolutions of Indian-white differences.

Political role playing was largely responsible. Elected officials courting votes saw little gain in a compromise solution to treaty fishing and probably devoted very little effort to the matter. For the governor and attorney general, gill nets and Indians could hardly have been high priorities. They played to the public when the opportunity came their way.

The apocalyptic quality of the rhetoric limited the chances for compromise. State leaders repeatedly predicted disaster if Indian fishing continued: violence, a ruined fishery, destruction of an important tourist attraction, and loss of hundreds of millions of dollars. Oversimplified and terribly exaggerated, these dire predictions lacked factual support, but they prevented a reasoned solution to the dispute. As the public came to believe the rhetoric, support for the Indians or even compromise with them became politically risky.

And some Michigan policy makers, particularly Howard

State Efforts to Regain Control   117

Tanner and a few men around him, had too strong an emotional commitment to the sport-fishing industry, which they had built, to accept the legitimacy of Indian treaty claims. As long as Tanner remained head of the Department of Natural Resources, he would be a powerful opponent of treaty fishing. The strength of his reactions to treaty fishing is understandable perhaps. Tanner had created one of the great sport fisheries in the world. With courage and foresight, he had turned an alewife-plagued water wasteland into a wonderfully attractive and productive fishery. If anything, he was too involved, too emotionally bound to his work to deal calmly and effectively with the issue.

Governor William Milliken did not run for reelection in 1982, and Howard Tanner left with Milliken. The men who replaced them had no emotional commitments to the sport fishery and no bad feelings toward their Indian adversaries. Judge Noel Fox left the bench in 1983. His support for Indian rights had dampened state enthusiasm for federal court. But now he was gone and his replacement, Judge Richard Enslen, could not be easily categorized. With Fox, Milliken, and Tanner gone, the state could proceed pragmatically and vigorously defend its legal interests.

Some new attorneys began to play significant roles at about the same time these other changes took place. Elizabeth Valentine took over the state's case when it seemed that the allocation issue might go to trial, and Ted Swift and Steve Schultz were allowed to enter the fray on behalf of sport fishermen. The skills of these three attorneys balanced Bruce Greene's, and so the weight of legal expertise no longer favored the Indians.

Eventually these new people and changed circumstances produced a settlement in which state and sport-fishing interests prevailed. Unwittingly, the state had managed to waste time until favorable circumstances presented themselves. Seen from such a point of view, the victory seems historically determined—impossible during the Carter presidency and a foregone conclusion during the Reagan years. Despite botching its opportunities, the state would have other chances for a favorable out-of-court settlement as long as Ronald Reagan remained president. Early in 1981, Secretary Watt had instructed Deputy Undersecretary of the Interior William P. Horn to press for such a settlement.

As chief negotiator, Horn brought much-needed savvy to the conflict. Trained as a lawyer, Horn used his wide-ranging experience and political astuteness to pressure the Indians and the state to talk out their differences. He began by discussing the issues with his associates at the Department of the Interior, a sprawling bureaucracy that comprised all the interests competing for Great Lakes fish—sportsmen, conservationists, and Indians. Horn did not have to go far for advice, much of it simply reflecting the dispute itself. But Horn found a well-informed and relatively neutral expert in Joseph Kutkuhn, the director of the Great Lakes Fish Laboratory in Ann Arbor. Horn and Kutkuhn talked at length about the issues and then drafted a settlement plan.[26]

Horn's plan sought to attain three fundamental objectives: accommodation of Indian rights; protection of the fishery, especially lake trout; and minimization of conflict among the user groups. Horn believed these objectives could be achieved by a zonal allocation of the fishery.

Speaking at a May 1982 Republican fund-raiser in Manistee, Michigan, Interior Secretary Watt revealed Horn's settlement plan, which, he said, all the parties had accepted in concept. Outside the fund-raiser, demonstrators ridiculed Watt's environmental policies, but the plan William Horn had devised certainly focused on conservation and restoring the lake trout. Horn divided the Great Lakes treaty waters into four types of zones: sport fishing, Indian commercial fishing, a large lake trout refuge along the Manitou–Beaver Island chain, and a few small areas where Indians could fish with trap nets. Indians would be allowed to gillnet only in tribal zones, primarily located in the north. By reserving southern waters, including most of the "gold coast" area between Empire and Cross

State Efforts to Regain Control 119

Village, for sport fishing, Horn had protected the lucrative tourist fishery and removed Indian fishermen from much of the water in which they had treaty rights. In lieu of the southern fishing grounds, the Indians would be given the grounds formerly controlled by big-boat white commercial fishermen. White trap-netters would be bought out. Horn indicated that all parties accepted the principles underlying the agreement, but longtime observers noted that many problems remained unresolved.[27]

Horn's plan set a wise course but a risky one unless the negotiators took up issues that Horn had chosen to suppress temporarily. The plan made no effort to restructure the fishery—to ameliorate common-goods problems, update outmoded management techniques, or foster local controls. Nor did it carefully define an administrative system to govern the fishery. To be sure, these sorts of issues were better ignored at first until a general allocation of the fishery had taken place. Horn had sensibly buried these problems for a while. But they were not going to go away, and the chance for reform would vanish once a settlement took place.[28]

Horn's plan never gained wide support and within a few weeks the state revealed an alternative proposal. Nevertheless, Horn's concepts now dominated the field; zones, Indians to gillnet primarily in the north where they would take over the commercial fishery formerly controlled by whites, sport fishing in the south, lake trout rehabilitation in refuges. These concepts shaped the negotiations over the next three years. and the support the Department of the Interior had given to sport-fishing interests encouraged their spokesmen to press for out-of-court negotiations.[29]

Ted Swift and Steve Schultz, attorneys for the Grand Traverse Area Sport Fishing Association, realized the potential for a negotiated victory. In the spring of 1981, Swift had advised Governor Milliken to negotiate a settlement since he believed the state stood little chance of a legal victory. Swift told the governor that Michigan would lose in the United States Supreme Court. But attorney general Frank Kelley contended that negotiations were, as he put it, "selling out" his efforts to win the case. Milliken should have acted upon Swift's correct assessment but, instead, allowed Kelley to control the situation. By 1982, the accuracy of Swift's view was apparent and the state began to negotiate seriously.[30]

Issued shortly after Horn's, the state settlement plan was similar. Indeed, from this time on, all settlement plans were similar. Responding to the state's proposal on behalf of his Indian clients, Bruce Greene said that "conceptually, the plan appears to have some merit . . . perhaps the potential for being a very attractive resolution of the problems." In other words, the Indians were willing to talk, and the structure of the plan was acceptable even if the details were not.[31]

William Horn kept people talking and in August 1982 he gathered Indian and state spokesmen in Ann Arbor for what he hoped would be the final negotiations. Beginning with a revised version of the state plan, Horn gradually shaped an agreement in principle, which state and Indian negotiators discussed for three days and finally endorsed. Horn had spoken with one party and then another and another, making adjustments as he went, until he had a document everyone accepted. It was a remarkable achievement, considering the mutual antipathy of the parties.[32]

Like the plan Watt had proposed in Manistee, Horn's Ann Arbor agreement allocated the fishery according to zones. It set limits on the total number of fish to be caught in each zone or on the total amount of fishing effort per zone. The agreement was to be administered by a Technical Advisory Committee composed of federal, state, and tribal representatives.[33]

A cautious optimism prevailed in the weeks after the Ann Arbor agreement was signed. Joseph Lumsden, chairman of the Sault tribe said that he could "see the end of a 10-year battle and a chance to settle the issues permanently. And I feel we should." Stuart Freeman, assistant attorney general for Michi-

State Efforts to Regain Control 121

gan, indicated that "the governor's office and the tribal leaders seem confident of agreement." But Freeman also pointed out that a lot of work remained before a final settlement could be put in place.[34]

Troubles soon surfaced. Indians began arguing among themselves. The Grand Traverse band worried about protecting its fishermen's rights to gillnet near their homes, which bordered the "gold coast." The attorney for the band, William Rastetter, fretted over the agreement's effects on nonsignatory Indians and about its elimination of claims to inland hunting and fishing rights. Stewart Freeman indicated that the state needed to consult with leaders of conservation and sportsmen's groups and with legislators and administrators. White commercial fishermen filed suit to protect their businesses.

And problems existed within the agreement. Consisting mostly of generalities, the document had to be wholly rewritten and the details put in place before it could be submitted to the disputants and the court for final acceptance. And the details were important since they determined how much of the fishery was allocated to each group. Horn had also made a mistake in not committing the parties to a schedule for revision of the document, discussion of the revision, and final acceptance. Lacking a binding schedule, people put things off. Nothing got done, and before long the opportunity for settlement vanished.

Toward the end of the August negotiations in Ann Arbor, after three days of nonstop bargaining, Stewart Freeman and the other state participants had told William Horn that they lacked authority to sign the agreement that was nearing completion. Tired and frustrated, Horn lost his temper and launched into a tirade against the state's duplicity. He told the state people that they had better get such authority immediately. Sullenly, they complied, but Horn had made enemies. During the fall, as state foot-dragging increased and the agreement began to unravel, Horn wondered if he hadn't pushed too hard. Later, though, he came to believe that state leaders had not wanted to settle and had never intended to abide by the Ann Arbor agreement. Horn was undoubtedly right.[35]

Bruce Greene eventually wrote a consent decree based upon the Ann Arbor agreement, which the state promptly turned down. Attorneys for the United States revised Greene's document, but by this time Michigan voters had elected James Blanchard governor, thereby creating political uncertainties. Horn's Ann Arbor agreement in principle died in January 1983.[36]

State-licensed commercial fishermen caught too many fish in 1982, and they resumed overfishing in the spring of 1983. Assuming that in the long run the Indians would take over the lakes, they grabbed quick profits. Knowing that seasonal closures were in the offing, they raced the Indians to net as many fish as fast as they could. Indians could not compete as prices plummeted in the fish-glutted market. Tribal leaders realized that they could not negotiate endlessly. In November 1983 the tribes petitioned the federal district court to allocate the fishery resource because the present system did not "yield sufficient fish to meet the tribal needs."[37]

Bruce Greene had already begun to prepare for a trial that would divide the resource. He confronted a much more difficult legal situation than in phase 1 since he had few legal precedents to guide him. He also had to contend now with a newly troublesome Grand Traverse band, which had begun to define a separate position for itself. As his motion to allocate indicated, Greene needed to establish the extent of tribal needs and to specify how many fish the tribes needed to satisfy those needs. In his response to Greene's motion, attorney Steve Schultz pointed out that Greene also needed to develop an actual plan for allocation—a practical method for dividing the fishery. But officially, the Indians had no plan in mind yet.

Lawyers fought paper wars through the spring and summer of 1984, but in the fall Judge Richard Enslen, who had replaced

State Efforts to Regain Control

Noel Fox, seized control of the case and headed it toward resolution. Enslen had complicated the case by allowing white commercial fishermen and several sport-fishing organizations to participate as friends of the court, since their interests in the fishery were unrepresented. Yet if fairness dictated admitting them to the dispute, practicality did not. The case had become extraordinarily tangled, and legal precedent did not point the way out. Judge Enslen had created a dilemma for himself.

Seeking a solution to this and many other cases that involved important and not easily settled issues, Judge Enslen had become interested in forms of alternative dispute resolution. He consulted with attorneys in the *United States v. Michigan* case and with associates experienced in the use of special masters in complex litigation. None of these lawyers warned him that alternative dispute resolution often worked to the advantage of more powerful litigants. During a three-day conference in Aspen, Colorado, Enslen spoke with Francis E. McGovern, a highly recommended and successful master, who quickly became Enslen's choice to manage the case for trial and simultaneously to seek a negotiated end to the dispute.

In a long letter to the *United States v. Michigan* attorneys, dated June 28, 1984, Enslen recommended McGovern and appealed for other nominations. He pointed out that the master must be a "lawyer highly skilled in mediation, conciliation, etc. . . . [who] ought to be a person unfamiliar with the fishery problem in Michigan, and perhaps unfamiliar with fishery problems in general." But realizing the importance of well-disciplined intelligence, Enslen emphasized the need for a special expert in fisheries to serve along with the master. Unfortunately the parties did not see the need for a fisheries expert, and Judge Enslen's advice was not taken. No one, therefore, spoke for the fish or the fishery when McGovern won out over other nominees and became special master. *United States v. Michigan* was headed toward settlement under the control of a man skilled in getting people to say yes.[38]

CHAPTER EIGHT
With Utmost Good Faith?

Within six months of his appointment as special master, Francis McGovern had negotiated a settlement of *United States* v. *Michigan*. Similar to William Horn's 1982 Ann Arbor agreement, McGovern's Sault Ste. Marie agreement split the fishery into zones, with the state dominating the southern waters and Indians controlling the northern commercial fishery. Overall, the Sault Ste. Marie agreement favored white interests, the state of Michigan, and big-boat Indian gill-netters, though the plan was complex and its outcome uncertain.

On March 28, 1985, exactly 149 years after the signing of the Treaty of Washington and a month before *United States* v. *Michigan* was scheduled for trial, Indians and whites agreed to allocate the fishery without going to court. After three days of continuous talks at Sault Ste. Marie and several months of accelerated discovery, the weary disputants signed a consent order that divided the fishery and ended, it was hoped, more than a dozen years of litigation.

Judge Richard Enslen called the Sault Ste. Marie agreement "virtually a miracle," but actually it developed naturally out of Horn's work in Ann Arbor and some advantages that accrued to McGovern as a special master. As the court's agent, McGovern had coercive power. He pushed a rapid-fire discovery schedule to wear down the attorneys. He forced negotiators to acquire power to make binding agreements on the spot. For further motivation, he had the threat of an unpredictable trial lacking clear precedents.[2]

As a special master, Francis McGovern operated without rules or guidelines. Alternative dispute resolution has no legally defined procedures; McGovern set his own standards for a "good" settlement. He had no interest in restructuring the fishery or shifting the locus of its benefits. He considered Judge Enslen his primary constituency, and he curried favor with the judge. Critics of alternative dispute resolution point out that situations of this sort often play into the hands of powerful interests at the expense of weaker ones in a context where everyday morality prevails.[3]

Inasmuch as all the parties had agreed in 1982 to Horn's Ann Arbor plan, the disputants knew that the final settlement would most likely be a zonal allocation. McGovern attributed his successes to a computer simulation, the Lake Wasota Fishing Rights Game, which had helped him to devise a settlement scheme. But everyone involved in the conflict had previously accepted the principles around which the fishery should be divided. Horn had done the tough work before McGovern had shown up. McGovern simply needed a way to get people's binding signatures. Together with coercive power, he had something to sweeten the pot, money.

Rumors of money had floated among the tribes ever since the state had offered to buy up the Indian's treaty rights. McGovern's expense account allowed him to entertain the litigants—dinner, drinks, lodging—and to find out what it would take to get them to sign. During these meetings, McGovern mentioned a financial arrangement that might facilitate the upcoming negotiations. Sometime before formal negotiations were to begin in late March, McGovern approached William Horn and a spokesperson for the state, probably Ronald Skoog, director of the Department of Natural Resources, and asked them to come to the negotiations prepared to pay money to the tribes as part of a settlement—to come "with some money in their pockets," as Horn later put it.[4]

The Sault Ste. Marie agreement obligated Michigan and the federal government each to pay the tribes $855,000 and to contribute $1.5 million each to a trust fund, whose income was to be used for Indian fishery development. At 10 percent interest the trust fund would generate $4.5 million during its fifteen-year life-span. Overall, the tribes would get roughly $6.2 million in additional monies if they signed, but nothing if they refused. Lead negotiator for the Indians, Joseph Lumsden, testified under oath that he would not have signed if the settlement had not included money.[5]

McGovern later described this strategy as an outcome of his computer-simulated fishing-rights game. Here's McGovern's description, which, though tedious, deserves careful reading:

A program was run to determine if any scenario would satisfy each party's minimum priorities. When the game was limited to the case's legal issues, no negotiated outcome seemed possible. If, however, the issues were expanded to include other items that might be subject to negotiation, some solutions might satisfy the hypothetical minimum interests of the parties. A court, for example, was limited to interpreting the treaty in perpetuity; an agreement by the parties could be for a term of years. *A negotiated disposition, unlike a typical court decision, could also include provisions for plantings of fish, monetary payments, and market development.* When these and other issues were added to the computer, there emerged combinations of components which indicated different possible solutions where agreement was feasible.

As originally designed, the scorable game had another, more important function. *Its primary purpose was as an educational tool, not just to provide specific answers, but to teach the parties how to negotiate.* If all of the key decision makers could play the game, typically separately, they might better appreciate their own and their adversaries' positions. Moreover, they might develop more confidence in their own abilities and power as negotiators. The negotiation prong thus became an educational and behavioral task, aimed at educating the parties concerning the potential for maximizing their own interests, developing their strategic negotiating capacity, expanding the roster of issues subject to bargaining, and softening communication and behavioral barriers to face-to-face negotiation. (My emphasis.)[6]

McGovern claims an educational role for his computer game and himself. He describes himself as a "cooperative participant." Surprisingly though, none of the parties recalls being educated by McGovern or playing his fishing-rights game and from the standpoint of the tribal leaders, McGovern's assertion seems ludicrous. McGovern educated himself. He found out what people wanted, who was strong, who weak, what sorts of personalities people had, and so on. He learned enough to gain a settlement, but he never helped people to negotiate their best interests.[7]

McGovern invited more than fifty men and women to Sault Ste. Marie on March 25, 1985. He allowed all the interested parties to participate, though most had only peripheral roles: a few comments or perhaps some expert advice about details. But these "noncentral" negotiators gained a sense of involvement that encouraged their future support.[8]

At the center, McGovern had representatives of the five governments; he called them the key decision makers: William Horn (United States), Elizabeth Valentine and Ronald Skoog (state of Michigan), Bruce Greene, Arnie Parrish, Jr., and Irma Parrish (Bay Mills Indian community), Joseph Lumsden (Sault tribe), Greg Bailey and Joseph Raphael (Grand Traverse band). The small group fashioned the agreement with advice from the outside. And on March 28, 1985, the negotiators signed the consent decree that allocated the fishery by zones.[9]

How are we to evaluate the agreement? Certainly its substance ought to provide the basic standard: Does it protect Indian treaty rights? Does it provide an opportunity for Indian fishermen to earn an adequate living? Does it lessen conflict among the user groups? Will the state be able to maintain its tourist-attracting sport fishery? Can the settlement be effectively administered? Who gained? Who lost? How will the settlement affect the Great Lakes fishery overall? Let us look at McGovern's evaluation first and then attempt a broader appraisal.

Writing in the *University of Chicago Law Review*, McGovern said that not enough time had elapsed to assess his plan but then tried to make a case for its successes. His analysis, which avoids the substance of the agreement, reveals his preoccupation with pleasing the judge and with economy. McGovern's primary objective, it appears, was to free the judge's calendar of what promised to be a long, expensive, and complex trial. "Economy" is McGovern's first standard by which to evaluate alternative dispute resolution and *United States* v. *Michigan*. In the introductory section of his article, roughly sixteen pages, McGovern mentions problems of efficiency and economy nineteen times, judicial overload six times, procedural fairness seven times, "justice" and injustice (note McGovern's quotation marks) three times. The frequencies clearly indicate his concerns.[10]

How well did McGovern succeed in his primary goal of saving the court time and money? He spend roughly two hundred thousand dollars, half of which went to him as compensation and expenses. He argued that such expenses should be balanced against reduced costs to the court in time and money, but McGovern did not specify the nature of these savings.[11] We may assume that his settlement forestalled a potentially long and complicated trial. Even so, a short trial took place in May 1985. Moreover, problems derived from ambiguities in the settlement have often usurped the court's time in the years since it went into effect. These problems will likely persist in view of the imprecision generally characterizing the language and concepts in the Sault Ste. Marie agreement. As of January 1990, more litigation loomed ahead, and the initial saving of time and money to the court may eventually disappear. Of course, we have no way of knowing what would otherwise have occurred.

Even if McGovern did save time and money for the court—and that is hardly indisputable—he did so by externalizing the problem, saving the judge's time by forcing other men and women to spend their time trying to untangle the settlement. The result was an administrative anomaly, an executive council charged with governing the fishery and resolving conflicts but virtually without power to do so. Composed of one representative from each of the tribes, from the Unites States Department of the Interior, and from the Michigan Department of Natural Resources, the executive council was to "meet and confer" about "the state of the fishery resource, the implementation of [the] agreement, expenditure of funds except as otherwise provided . . . and any dispute related hereto." But council members can only talk, not enforce, though the consent decree mentions that "the parties could adopt . . . [a] method of dispute resolution which establishes standards of review, additional powers and procedures, and assigns appropriate weight to decisions rendered."[12]

Disputes and problems quickly surfaced. How should the settlement monies be spent? Should they be distributed among the tribes? If so, how? Equally? On the basis of numbers of fishermen? Pounds of fish caught? If funds were not to be distributed to the tribes, what agency should manage the funds? Should a majority vote determine how to spend the money? Or should votes be unanimous? Should the Bureau of Indian Affairs manage the trust fund? What would happen to the trust fund when the settlement expired in fifteen years?

When the executive council first confronted such controversies and realized its impotence, the members understood that they needed some power to bind the parties, to coerce them. But lawyers for the various governments quickly conjured up worst-case scenarios, as lawyers often do. As a result, the executive council remains impotent, and serious disputes will have to go to court.[13]

An outsider who knew very little about the Great Lakes fishery. McGovern could not possibly have anticipated all the problems that arose in the succeeding years; probably no one could have. But he showed a notable inattention to detail when he failed even to have an expert stenographer present at Sault Ste. Marie, and he apparently had little interest in efficient administration. McGovern's genius lay in personal relations, not practicality.

One loophole in the agreement was especially perilous. It

was a proviso that "if there is surplus fish available for harvest that cannot otherwise be taken by treaty fishers," the state may reenter the commercial fishery in tribal waters. This arrangement encourages ecologically unsound fishing practices. Apparently, tribal fishermen must catch the total allowable catch year after year if they want to keep state-licensed netters out. The total allowable catch is a biologist's estimate of the *maximum* poundage of fish that can be caught in an area without damaging the reproductive capacity of the fish, not an estimate of the fish that *should* be caught. Because they feared that this provision would permit white commercial fishermen to reenter the fishery, the tribes felt it necessary to catch every allowable fish. Fortunately, the state has chosen to ignore this loophole and has not threatened to use it against the tribes. Nevertheless, the opportunity unfortunately remains, and the biological consequences of taking the total allowable catch year after year are not explored. A long trial will take place if the state decides to press the issue, a losing situation whatever the outcome.[14]

In his article McGovern does not define a standard by which to judge fairness. Instead, he briefly discusses expedited discovery and negotiations. He says that "the negotiations . . . afforded significant opportunity for maximizing the values of dignity, autonomy, and participation." He indicates that Elizabeth Valentine, attorney for the state, may have suffered some disadvantage in discovery. Actually, McGovern had scheduled discovery so Valentine could not possibly attend all the sessions. She commented to the *Legal Times:* "I'm not sure you get the best results when you put people in a pressure cooker." Hasty discovery "would have made for a much longer trial and . . . the settlement is not as comprehensive as it could have been had the parties had more time in discovery to gather information on biological questions."[15]

McGovern's discussion of other fairness issues is just as sketchy, though he was responsible for establishing equitable procedures. He indicates briefly that some critics of alternative dispute resolution believe that "courts equalize power imbalances while ADR maintains relative power positions, thus favoring the 'haves.'" In other words, the have-nots find it difficult to defend their interests under ADR and need help negotiating. McGovern put this important insight into footnote 45. In the text, he notes that opponents of alternative dispute resolution believe that "parties who have less power and society as a whole with its interest in the information that disputes generate will be disadvantaged by private dispute resolution." Then, McGovern drops the matter of fairness.[16]

Familiar though he was with the power inequalities of alternative dispute resolution, McGovern appears to have ignored the critics' warnings. For example, he did not establish procedures to redress imbalances among negotiators, nor did he discuss such procedures in his article. He talks about educating the parties to the suit but does not explain when or how he did so or to what end. Actually he seems not to have educated at all but rather to have simply put together negotiators who had vastly different capacities to defend their interests.

McGovern designated ten people as the key decision makers at Sault Ste. Marie. There were four highly trained attorneys (McGovern, Bruce Greene, Elizabeth Valentine, and William Horn), a widely experienced public administrator (Ronald Skoog), a clever and very bright Indian leader (Joseph Lumsden), and four inexperienced Indians (Joseph Raphael, Greg Bailey, Arnie Parrish, Jr., and Irma Parrish). These people had vastly different abilities to defend their interests.[17]

Personal connections guided the negotiations as well as interests. Elizabeth Valentine played a negligible role since several of these men refused to take her seriously, in part, it would appear, because she is a woman. The four inexperienced Indians had little influence because they lacked the skills to look after their constituents' interests. Raphael, an able politician among his people, even left the proceedings to patch up some difficulties between his band and the Bureau of Indian Affairs. McGovern, Greene, Skoog, and Horn provided the crucial connection. Horn and Skoog had established a congenial and successful working relationship in Alaska. McGovern, Greene, and Horn shared values common among high-powered, cosmopolitan attorneys. Horn and McGovern got along well and worked closely together to bring about a settlement. McGovern and Greene liked each other and admired each other's skills. These connections guided the bargain they struck with Joseph Lumsden, the only Indian skilled enough to advance his interests. Predictably, the other four Indians could not protect their constituents, the small-boat gill-netters and the Indian fishermen in highly developed tourist areas such as Grand Traverse Bay. The Sault Ste. Marie agreement took important fishing opportunities away from both groups and gave them little in return.[18]

Was it fair to put people of such unequal abilities together in negotiation? It bears repeating that McGovern made no effort to redress these imbalances. His claim that he trained people lacks foundation. A well-read student of negotiation and an experienced special master, McGovern had to have known that he had selected negotiators of unequal skills. In his haste to please Judge Enslen and get the agreement the judge wanted, McGovern apparently lost sight of his obligation to ensure fair procedures to everyone.

It seems obvious that alternative dispute resolution ought to be regulated. At the very least, a special master should be required by law to tell the parties that successful negotiation requires well-honed skills and to advise them to hire a professional negotiator if they lack training or confidence. Nor should the master be able to pick the negotiators for each party, as McGovern did. The parties should be allowed to chose who will represent them without regard to the master's wishes. Certainly, it would be unfair if a federal judge selected the people who would organize and present the cases of the parties to a suit, particularly if the judge chose attorneys of such unequal skills as the men and women whom McGovern picked.

Alternative dispute resolution should offer the same promise as the court: a fair chance to defend your interests. Neither court nor ADR can promise justice or equality. Combatants—whether lawyers in court or negotiators in dispute resolution—will always be somewhat unequal. But McGovern did not afford the Grand Traverse or Bay Mills groups a fair chance, and for this unfortunate situation he must assume primary responsibility.

McGovern might have partially redressed inequalities at Sault Ste. Marie by making expert negotiators available to the parties for training and advice before the session began. These experts could have helped the less-experienced parties sharpen their negotiating skills, and they should have been present during the final sessions, if not actually in the central group, then at least nearby for consultation.

Yet despite procedural inequalities, we must judge the settlement by its substance. Did the Ottawas and Chippewas get a fair deal? Or did some Native Americans win while most lost, as would at first seem to be the case? Let us see if we can use a "moderate standard of living" to measure fairness, as the federal courts have sometimes done. Did the settlement provide enough fish for Indian fishermen to earn a modest living?

The only detailed evidence available was gathered by Charles Cleland, the anthropologist who had testified for the plaintiff in the first phase of the trial. The data in the report Cleland prepared at Bruce Greene's behest seem relatively accurate, even though they are based upon survey techniques that encourage bias and make them potentially untrustworthy. Cleland faced a difficult problem trying to collect complex economic information from often unlettered fishermen. He garnered his evidence using face-to-face interviews that usually involved people who knew one another and, in any case, ensured a lack of anonymity. Furthermore, the interviewers were instructed to tell the fishermen that they were gathering data to be used in the fishing rights litigation. However practical or even necessary, Cleland's strategies violated generally accepted standards for collecting survey data.

Cleland identified 102 Indian fishermen—actually the heads of fishing crews, who had to file catch reports with the tribes, so the total number of fishermen, including helpers, part timers, and subsistence fishers was undoubtedly much higher, perhaps 200 in all, but it is hard to be sure. Sixteen "big" fishermen caught 56.5 percent of the fish and had incomes that averaged more than $24,600 each in 1981. Thirty-six "small" fishermen caught 38 percent of the fish and averaged $8,300 in income. Fifty "very small" fishermen took 5.5 percent of the catch and averaged a loss. The settlement would have to provide enough additional fish to raise the incomes of the eighty-six small and very small fishermen to a moderate level. The big fishermen already had acceptable incomes.[19]

Let us assume a constant number of fishermen, that the wholesale price of fish averaged fifty cents per pound, that small and very small fishermen paid crew shares of 25 percent, that big boats paid wages averaging 30 percent of their gross, and that big and small fishermen continued to catch fish in the same proportions (small, 43.5 percent; big, 56.5 percent). And let us arbitrarily set fifteen thousand dollars as a modest income—a low level but roughly the same as the mean income of Chippewa County in the eastern upper peninsula. Given these assumptions, how many additional pounds of fish would the settlement have to provide to allow all the Indian fishermen to earn moderate incomes?[20]

The thirty-six small fishermen who averaged $8,300 in income needed enough fish for an increase of $6,700, roughly 13,400 pounds each, plus 4,600 pounds to pay their help or 18,000 pounds each for an increased group total of 648,000 pounds (18,000 × 36). Following the same process for the fifty very small fishermen (and counting their starting income as zero), we would need 40,000 pounds per fishermen, for a total of 2 million pounds (40,000 × 50). Overall, the small and very small fishermen needed an increase of 2,648,000 pounds to gross fifteen thousand dollars each. But if the big fishermen were going to catch 56.5 percent of the fish, the settlement would have to increase the tribal catch by several million pounds to allow the small fishermen to earn modest livings unless, of course, the big fishermen's total catch was limited, a politically unthinkable solution at the time.

Obviously such rough calculations should be viewed with great caution, but most of my assumptions are conservative. It therefore seems safe to assume that the tribes needed several million pounds more fish. Such gains would destroy the fishery, however. The total allowable catch set for whitefish in 1985 was 6.8 million pounds, of which the tribes were already catching 3.2 million pounds. If the Indians took all the whitefish in 1985, they would only gain about 3.6 million pounds, well short of their needs, and the agreement obligated them to stop netting within a few years in productive waters such as Hammond Bay, where they took 529,000 pounds in 1985. It is hard, really, to see how enough fish could be found to provide tribal fishermen a moderate living.[21]

People close to the controversy knew there were not enough fish to go around. Just prior to entering the Sault Ste. Marie negotiations, each of the parties submitted allocation plans to the court. Though these were primarily negotiating postures, not necessarily to be taken seriously, Peter Steketee, attorney for Michigan United Conservation Clubs, noted that all the plans contained serious flaws. He sent a long position paper to the court and attorneys of record on March 19, 1985, six days before negotiations began. Steketee indicated that unless the tribes restructured the fishery and cut back the number of fishermen, no reasonable settlement was available. "A modest standard of living for . . . [tribal] fishermen is unavailable without limited entry. Even if 100% of the fishery's resources . . . were allocated to the tribes, the harvestable surplus would not be adequate to assure a modest living to all of the Indian fishermen." Steketee was right, of course.[22]

The Sault Ste. Marie agreement squeezed out increases for the Indians but nothing in the neighborhood of several million pounds seemed likely. Biologists estimated that the tribes would realize a net gain of only about 500,000 pounds of whitefish. Other increases would have to come from expanded fisheries in salmon, walleye, yellow perch, and a restored put-grow-take lake trout fishery in Whitefish Bay. These problematic fisheries depended primarily on state plantings, which were to begin in 1985. Stocking, especially the annual planting of 500,000 salmon for the tribes, might generate substantial long-term benefits. But no commercial market existed for Great Lakes salmon at the time, and these fishes have accumulated toxic contaminants in the past. So we will have to wait to see about this enhanced fishery. But small fishermen who needed to lift their nets regularly could hardly wait to see how things turned out. Long term for them is often a few days until the next lift of their nets.[23]

The Sault Ste. Marie agreement offered little to the needy Indian small-boat fishermen, many of whom dropped out of the fishery in the next two years. By the count of tribal biologist William Eger, the number of small boaters fell from 103 in 1984 before the settlement to 76 in December 1986, a decrease of 26 percent. These figures differ from Cleland's. Nevertheless, we can be sure that many small fishermen dropped out of the fishery after the settlement.[24]

In 1986 the Indian fishermen using large boats took 61 percent of the catch, and poundage increased by 12 percent. The total increase was 463,600 pounds, or almost 15,500 pounds for each of thirty big boats. At the estimated price of 50 cents per pound, each boat grossed about $39,250, or $7,750 more than in 1984. Small boats, however, grossed on average only about $10,000, a meager income when we consider crew shares of 25 percent and other expenses.[25]

Bay Mills Indian fishermen protested the settlement as soon as they saw it. They had lost two productive and relatively safe fishing grounds and gained very little in return. A direct democracy in which all adults have equal say, the community held three long meetings and then voted to reject the Sault Ste. Marie agreement. In its place, the community offered a plan in which the Indians would get 50 percent of the commercial catch in each statistical area throughout the treaty waters.

United States v. *Michigan* went back to federal court in May 1985 before Judge Richard Enslen with all the parties aligned against Bay Mills and in support of the Sault Ste. Marie agreement. Assisted by another Native American Rights Fund attorney, Bruce Greene handled the case for Bay Mills. He had little chance of overturning a settlement that everyone else, including the judge, wanted, especially since he could not argue for a modest standard of living based upon Cleland's improperly collected data.[26]

The trial centered on whether the agreement would provide enough fish for the small-boat fishermen. The allowable catches in the new Indian commercial zones indicated a small overall increase in the potential whitefish catch, but Bay Mills contended that the far-offshore fishing grounds in these new areas were dangerously unsuitable for small boats. Gill-net tug fishermen from the Sault tribe would catch these fish. Joseph Lumsden emerged victorious here, though at small cost to the state, which did not care about the white commercial trap-netters who would lose their right to fish these grounds.

The following spring, in March 1986, the Sault tribe ran a full-page advertisement in the tribal paper announcing eight new licenses for boats over twenty-five feet. Six of the eight licenses (four gill-net tugs and two trap-net operations) were centered in the new Indian commercial zones around Manistique and Naubinway—precisely the grounds that the Bay Mills small-boat fishermen said they could not safely work. The other two licenses were for trap-netting in St, Ignace waters, where Bay Mills fishermen frequently netted in the spring.[27]

Debates at the trial over fish supplies and the potential Indian commercial catch depended upon error-prone data. No one knows for sure how many fish of which species inhabit the lakes. Assessments, total allowable catches, and catch reports are all untrustworthy, though for different reasons. But during the trial, the parties tossed numbers back and forth without regard to their origins or their potential for error.

With the focus on fish supplies and size of the Indian commercial catch, no one said much about the sport fishery or tourism. Attorneys for the state of Michigan and sport fishermen squelched efforts to reveal the background of the settlement, what interests were traded upon and which compromised. Fearing litigation, the state apparently did not want to reveal why it had given away the northern commercial fishery in order to regain full control of the lucrative southern sport-fishing waters.[28]

Scott McElroy, Bruce Greene's associate, tried, nevertheless, to reveal the motives that produced the agreement. McElroy asked William Horn, who was being considered for appointment as assistant secretary of the interior, if he would benefit politically from the support of sportsmen's groups: "Do you think that it would be useful to you in obtaining the position of Assistant Secretary to have the support of MUCC?" Horn never gave a direct answer, but clearly the support would be most advantageous. Michigan United Conservation Clubs had good connections in Reagan's Department of the Interior. Tom Washington, head of MUCC, was a close associate of James Watt and served on Watt's informal advisory council. Ever the politician, Horn rejected political motives on his part and insisted that he supported the settlement on its merits including "reduced social conflict."[29]

After a brief trial, Judge Richard Enslen dismissed the Bay Mills allocation plan and accepted the Sault Ste. Marie agreement. Of the prime sport-fishing waters, only the far northern Les Cheneaux Islands and a tiny area off the Leelanau Peninsula would remain open to gillnetting after 1990. Drawing a boundary around the sport fishery, the settlement pushed the Indians north into waters the state considered unimportant.

Remarkably, just six years before, Judge Noel Fox had anticipated such a situation. Because the historic Chippewas and Ottawas had fished "extensively over the ceded area, going where the fish were to be found," Judge Fox warned that the Indians' right to fish should not be "limited . . . to imaginary and unrealistic boundaries."[30]

Overall, it appears that alternative dispute resolution did not defend Chippewa-Ottawa treaty rights as well as trial in federal court would have done, for in court treaties are interpreted as the Indians would have understood them. It is difficult to see what modifications of alternative dispute resolution could offer the same protections. In this case, any determination of "adequate defense" of treaty rights probably must be measured subjectively. Who gained and who lost? Did the Indians give away too much, especially waters suitable for small-boat gillnetting?

The Indians conceded the right to gillnet in almost all the inshore waters around the lower peninsula, a crucial victory for the state of Michigan, which regained control over these money-making sport-fishing areas. The state got what it wanted and gave up only a commercial fishery for which it had little concern. Sport-fishing interests got what they wanted, too, except along the north shore of Lakes Michigan and Huron. The state had simply sacrificed the Bays de Noc and the Cheneaux Islands to get full control in the south. Small-boat Indian fishermen lost out, as did those who lived in the lower peninsula. For the most part, the treaty rights to fish with gill nets in sheltered bays and in lower peninsula home waters were traded away for open waters in the north suitable only for big boats. Such results grew predictably from the context in Sault Ste. Marie, which allowed the stronger interests to prevail and failed to offer the weaker interests a fair opportunity to defend themselves.

CHAPTER NINE
What Should Be Done?

Faced with an abundance seemingly without limit, hoping to subdue the continent and civilize an untamed wilderness, lumbermen, fishermen, fur traders, and their Chippewa and Ottawa associates trapped animals for furs and slaughtered them for meat; they cut trees, exhausted land, and used up resources. Once the resources were depleted, non-Indians typically moved on, while Native Americans stayed behind, making a precarious living. Self-interest and market forces dictated exploitation. Conservation, seemingly unnecessary, made no economic sense.

The market especially fostered misuse of renewable resources such as fish, whose availability fluctuates seasonally. In spring and fall fish are easily caught, the market is flooded, and prices plummet. Fishermen have no choice but to increase their catch, pushing prices lower until fishing becomes unprofitable. The market demands excessive fishing—overuse of the resource—and brings few benefits to the fishermen, who cannot control supplies and, to survive, must produce more and more fish to get less and less money.

The fisherman's common-property predicament is ordinarily interpreted as a by-product of the natural qualities of the fish and their habitats, the market, and an innate human tendency toward self-centered materialism. Actually, of course, of the many factors that define the predicament, most are social and historical, not "natural" or "innate." Fisheries in other parts of the world have been organized according to various property systems that allocate the fish to different users, typically on the basis of residence, capital investment,

What Should Be Done? 141

or boat size and gear; many systems have been only indirectly concerned with protecting fish supplies, if at all.

John Cordell, a longtime student of property rights in inshore fisheries comparable to the Great Lakes, believes that "there is a disquieting tendency [today] to cast fishing rights primarily in terms of bioeconomic and technological considerations or efficiency priorities that are purportedly 'value free,' [and] justified by the ever-present danger of maritime degradation. These . . . 'management-oriented' perspectives frequently negate other, perhaps more fundamental human frameworks and needs." Cordell characterizes the common property description of inshore fisheries as an inaccurate paradigm reflecting historical Western European economic interests and legal traditions but now congenial to public managers and big-boat fishermen. According to Cordell, inshore fisheries throughout the world are allocated according to intricate but unofficial property systems devoted to ensuring local control, reducing conflict among small-boat fishermen, and encouraging social justice through equitable catch distributions. Because the rules defining these informal systems were seldom written down, scholars have only recently begun to appreciate their extent and power. By implication, Cordell indicates that we ought to understand these property systems and their functions before we put allocations in place that primarily seek to maximize profits through efficiency while ignoring other equally important objectives.

The open-access common-property system that prevails in the present-day Chippewa and Ottawa commercial fishery, and in the state-licensed fishery that preceded it, developed in response to the specific historical circumstances in which non-Indians organized the fishery to suit their profit-centered, individualist values. It allocates fish to big-boat fishermen and profits to middlemen, and it perpetuates poverty and dependency among most Indian fishermen. This situation derives from human choices, rather than seemingly immutable tendencies of fish or people, and it need not prevail. The Chippewas and Ottawas could restructure the fishery to accord with their traditions, which emphasized welfare of the group, generosity, and sharing.

Allocation issues need to be separated from those of conservation and efficient use. Prevalent in the public statements of fish and wildlife managers, this confusion pervades the thinking of policymakers and administrators, who often behave as if allocation to inefficient users, say hook-and-line fishermen as opposed to highly efficient gill-netters, represents the only way to safeguard a resource. Typically used to protect wildlife and fish, outlawing efficient harvest techniques, allocates the resource to people who have leisure time, but the resource could be equally well protected by other means. Desirable social purposes might be observed if individual quotas were imposed on a limited number of efficient users. Avoiding the confusion of resource protection and allocation, let us look at some protection matters first.

How can Michigan's Great Lakes fisheries best be protected? Since it involves biological issues, the question may seem better left for the experts to answer. But philosophical or policy decisions must be considered as well. After all, experts also have core values that shape their choices. Biology merely defines a range of alternatives among which we can choose; we need some principles to guide us.

Except for the whitefish, the Michigan Great Lakes are primarily a managed, put-grow-take fishery. Salmon, brown trout, walleye, and lake trout are all planted. The lakes are a huge fish farm, presently organized to maximize tourist-related profits. And plantings control harvests—you reap what you sow. In some respects, an artificial fishery of this sort has no conservation or protection issues whatsoever. All issues relate to allocation; how many fish will be planted and who will catch them.

This unnatural fishery came into being during the lamprey-alewife crisis of the 1960s. The policy made sense then as a solution for the alewife plague, but it makes less sense now

What Should Be Done?   143

that scientific research has revealed serious and continuing problems with water pollution and contamination of predator fish.

The put-grow-take fishery prospered famously under state guidance, and it created powerful economic and political interests. As long as those interests remain in control, they will seek to maintain the fishery as it is and will avoid examining the fundamental principles that guide their management decisions. To what ends should the fishery be managed? Could a naturally self-sustaining multispecies fishery be recreated? Should priority be given to such an effort? Could a natural fishery eventually sustain fish supplies near present levels? At what cost?

Neither the Department of Natural Resources nor those who fish for lake trout and salmon will seriously ask such questions as long as the present situation serves their interests. The Indians, the United States Fish and Wildlife Service, or Michigan citizens must press these matters, if they are to be raised at all. Ironically, James Watt and William Horn, often characterized as uninterested in environmental improvements, strongly encouraged the rebuilding of a natural fishery by insisting on lake trout refuges. None of the other combatants in *United States v. Michigan* has forced a broad public discussion of management objectives for the Great Lakes fishery. The rationale promoted by Howard Tanner and the DNR continues to prevail; that is, the state seeks the greatest monetary return on its investment, typically ignoring social and ecological costs. Any discussion must begin with the biology of the fishery. We must understand what management alternatives are available, what they offer, and what they would cost.

As of 1990, water pollution and contaminated fish represent the most serious problems confronting the fishery and its managers. From the beginning of the stocking program in the late 1960s, the flesh of Great Lakes trout and salmon contained so much toxic matter that large fish and those from more polluted waters exceeded federal Food and Drug Administration standards, could not be sold in interstate commerce, and represented a health threat—probably a serious one—to people who ate them. Throughout the 1970s, the Great Lakes Environment Contaminant Surveys revealed high levels of heavy metals (especially mercury) pesticides (primarily DDT) and PCBs in the large predator fish. The problem continues. Excessive levels of chlordane appeared in 1983. Later, it was toxaphene and dieldrin. In 1989, a study sponsored by the National Wildlife Federation found Lake Michigan trout and salmon to be dangerously contaminated. According to the study, eating these fish greatly increases the risk of contracting cancer.[2]

The DNR has never faced up to the public health issues raised by contaminated Great Lakes fish. Many studies have shown that consuming Great Lakes fish involves major health hazards, most notably, increased risks of cancer and birth defects. Though controversial, these studies were conducted by well-trained and respected experts who had no financial interest in the outcome of their research. The DNR has chosen only to issue a pamphlet containing vague warnings: "The presence of DDT and PCB pesticide and chemical residues in Great Lakes fish is of concern. Although still controversial, it is recommended by health authorities that the frequency and amounts of large Great Lakes fish eaten should be in moderation." In a booklet distributed with fishing licenses, the DNR warned pregnant women and nursing mothers not to eat lake trout, salmon, or steelhead from the Great Lakes and suggested other persons eat no more than half a pound of these fish per week.[3]

In a September 1981 article published in *Michigan Out-of-Doors*, the staff ecologist for the Michigan United Conservation Clubs, Wayne Schmidt, argued that DNR health advisories on fish were "inaccurate, out-of-date, and grossly incomplete." Schmidt believed that public officials were evad-

What Should Be Done? 145

ing responsibility for monitoring the quality of fish and that funding was insufficient for an adequate program comparable to one in Ontario, which checked about fifteen thousand fish each year from more than two hundred lakes and streams. According to Schmidt, the DNR had reasons not to publicize the toxicity of predator fish: "The DNR Fisheries Division faces a potential conflict of interest when confronted with aggressively publicizing fish contamination. Almost its entire budget comes from sales of fishing licenses and since last year $500,000 from the sale of salmon. If the PCB limit was dropped to two ppm, this salmon revenue would be lost."[4]

The Department of Natural Resources continues to spend state funds to produce predator fish, which health-conscious people refuse to eat because they contain threatening amounts of toxic chemicals. Actually, responsibility for the toxic fish rests not with the whole DNR, which is a large and unwieldy agency, but specifically with the Fisheries Division. Other divisions of the DNR and parts of the state government have fine environmental records, among the more progressive in the United States. Led by Governor James Blanchard and attorneys Stuart Freeman and Elizabeth Valentine, Michigan has vigorously prosecuted polluters and has tried to create a clean, healthful environment for its residents. Nevertheless, the Fisheries Division of the DNR is in the business of producing potentially dangerous food, nourishing tourist profits at the expense of human health. Should public money be spent to raise fish that should not be eaten? Why continue a put-grow-take fishery that creates health risks?

All users—Indian, white, commercial, sportsmen—from all states bordering the Great Lakes should immediately unite to control water pollution. It would not be an easy task since the mostly airborne pollutants such as toxaphene have to be traced and their sources eliminated. Nevertheless, improvements that generated clean water and nontoxic predator fish would increase the value of the fishery. Of course, a more valuable fishery would probably intensify allocation conflicts among the fish users. On what basis should the fish be allocated? And to whom?

The Sault Ste. Marie agreement, which split the fishery between white and Indian sovereigns, will define the overall allocation until the year 2000 and, most likely, afterwards. Within their exclusive zones, the sovereigns can use the fishery as they wish, give the fish and the fishery's benefits to whomever they want, provided they respect environmental limits, or at least appear to respect them. Nevertheless the state and the Indians have already decided how they wish to organize their fisheries without, it would seem, carefully considering the full range of alternatives.

The state remains locked into a profit-maximizing tourist-attracting sport fishery. The powerful and well-organized groups that support Great Lakes sport fishing would resist any policy changes and make them politically risky. Invariably given favorable media treatment, the Great Lakes fishery benefits politicians who support it. Many people fish, and no organized group is opposed to fishing, whereas fishing interests are well looked after by Michigan United Conservation Clubs, a Lansing-based sportsmen's lobby. The non-fishing public seems generally to approve of fishing as wholesome outdoor recreation and to see the Great Lakes fishery as a helpful economic stimulus. Therefore sport fishing offers politicians a chance to curry public favor without apparent risk: recall how William Milliken and other Michigan politicians turned the treaty-fishing controversy to their benefit.

The state ought to confront the health problems presented by its sport fishery and to face up to the apparent conflict between profit seeking and public health. Given its financial interests in the sport fishery, the DNR will probably never seriously deal with these issues, but the Department of Public Health certainly could, especially with some prodding from the governor or the Food and Drug Administration. People who wish to eat Great Lakes fish, especially lake trout, salm-

What Should Be Done?

on, and other predators, do not have enough information upon which to base informed choices about which fish to eat from which waters, or if they should eat Great Lakes fish at all. An angler who catches a large salmon and feeds it to his family or friends may well be poisoning them. At least he ought to know what toxic materials in what quantities the fish probably contains, if any. Someone needs to sponsor careful and extensive research into the health risks of eating Great Lakes fish and to publicize the results. The research should be conducted by an independent agency, relatively isolated from political pressure. A few years ago, during the height of the treaty-fishing controversy, state officials claimed the fishery was worth $500 million. Surely a few million of those dollars can be spent each year for health-related research and publicity.

There is nothing intrinsically wrong with the sport fishery as presently constituted, provided the health issues are investigated and publicized. Sport fishing benefits many people and represents a prudent financial investment, notwithstanding state puffery. But there is nothing intrinsically right about it either—no particular ecological wisdom, for example. The Great Lakes sport fishery results from a series of political decisions to spend public monies to nourish a resource and allocate it to a limited population, primarily middle-class white males. Spin-off benefits go to proprietors of tourist-related establishments. Interpreted in this manner, the choices that created the Great Lakes fishery and sustained it for nearly twenty-five years seem typical of many decisions that allocate resources to one group rather than another during the normal course of political affairs, are seldom talked about, but ought to be.

The Sault Ste. Marie agreement gives control of the northern Great Lakes fishery to three tribes, which have, with a few exceptions, allowed their members to operate an open-access commercial fishery in these highly productive waters. The tribes have not, as yet, restructured the fishery to eliminate those arrangements that allocate most benefits to middlemen, nearly all of whom are non-Indians and live outside the region in major urban centers. So, despite Indian control, the fishery provides terribly inadequate incomes for most tribal fishermen. It is a shame since it need not be the case.

The tribes should immediately make it possible for the fishermen to ship their own fish. Twice a week during the season, large refrigerated trucks pick up fish all over upper Michigan and deliver them to Chicago, New York, and other urban markets. These buyers pay more for the fish than the local wholesalers, as much as 40 percent more when prices are low. In 1987 the Grand Traverse band negotiated an annual contract to ship whitefish from the tribal trap-net business for ninety-three cents a pound year-round. In the spring of that year, the season when most whitefish are caught, independent trap-net fishermen from the Sault tribe were selling their fish to straits-area wholesalers for forty-five cents a pound, a dramatic illustration of the importance of marketing. A processing and storage facility in St. Ignace would be well located for a majority of the northern fishermen, who could then sell their fish directly as the Grand Traverse band has already begun to do. The Joint Tribal Management Authority could run the facility, using a percentage of the profits to cover overhead and pay a manager.[5]

The tribes should move into other marketing areas too. Large profits can be made retailing fish and hauling it to downstate markets in Lansing, Grand Rapids, and elsewhere. In August 1985 lake trout sold for sixty cents a pound in St. Ignace but brought a dollar a pound in the City Fish Company in Lansing. Merely hauling the fish two hundred miles brought a 67 percent increase in the return. Though unusually large, this price differential makes clear that the big money is made in the fishery by middlemen; if the tribes want to gain the full benefit from the fishery—more money and more jobs—they should get into the wholesale business as soon as possible.[6]

What Should Be Done?

The individual tribes could each begin to market fish on their own accounts, just as the Grand Traverse band began to do in 1982, but the management authority would probably be a more efficient market organizer, enabling all the Indians groups to share facilities, information, and costs. Refrigerated storage already exists in Bay Mills and Peshawbestown (Grand Traverse band). A similar facility could quickly be set up in St. Ignace, where the Sault tribe owns land and a well-equipped fish wholesaler recently closed. A central marketing office in St. Ignace could easily sell fish from all three reservations with some assistance from Bay Mills and Peshawbestown. Everyone would make more money.

Shipping, wholesaling, and retailing would bring increased shares of the fishery benefits to the Chippewas and Ottawas. A negotiated annual price would alter the old exploitative market system that forces fishermen to sell at tragically low prices—dressed whitefish wholesaled for twenty-five cents per pound during the 1985 spring run, for example. If the Indians take them, these initiatives will go a long way toward ameliorating Native American economic difficulties, but only if they are accompanied by some sort of profit-sharing system and fair allocation between big and small boats. Otherwise, most benefits will accrue to a very few people, just as they did before.

Most Indian fishermen continue to earn meager incomes working from small boats with a few gill nets. Some of these men fish full time, some have other jobs, but all struggle to gain a little more money to support their families. The tribes should address the needs of these small fishermen, since there are apparently not enough fish to provide all of them with modest incomes unless the Indians regain access to Hammond Bay and similar areas. The tribes should set aside specific inshore waters for the exclusive use of the small-boat fishermen. These should be historically productive grounds where men can fish from small boats in relative safety. Big boats, especially gill-net tugs, should be excluded from these areas and be forced to fish offshore or in less protected waters. Such controls are typical of many fisheries in the world.

The tribes must face up to the allocation problem and determine whether or not they want most of the fishery's benefits to fall to a handful of big fishermen, as seems to be the situation now and has commonly been the case in the past. A few big-boat fishermen could net the total allowable catch in most zones and could increase the overall poundage caught by Indian fishermen. A few big fishermen could be more easily policed than many small ones. And big boats could bring immediate financial benefits to a tribe, which takes a share of the catch from each new big-boat licensee. But allocation to small boats, which provides more jobs for more people, makes great sense in an area like upper Michigan where Indians have had so much trouble finding suitable work. A man could earn a decent living in a limited-entry small-boat fishery that had exclusive use of safe inshore fishing grounds. The tribes should take the long view and foster the small-boat fishery by controlling the big boats. Besides, there are better ways to make money in the fishery than taking a cut of an expanded big-boat catch.

If the tribes limited the number of small-boat fishermen, allocated certain waters to their exclusive use, and controlled the large boats, they could probably show that many fishermen could not earn a modest living in the waters the Indians presently control. The tribes would then have a legitimate basis for reclaiming some of the waters given up in the Sault Ste. Marie agreement, which could now be set aside for small boats only. Given the preferences expressed by Bay Mills fishermen at the 1985 minitrial, Hammond Bay would seem appropriate for immediate reacquisition.

As of the summer of 1988, the Sault tribe had taken several well-conceived initiatives designed to ensure it an independent position in the fishery. Though possibly flawed in detail, the tribal plan has merit since it will increase Indian autonomy

What Should Be Done?

by creating a tribally controlled put-grow-take salmon fishery in northern Lake Huron. The tribe recently purchased the former Ponderosa Fishery near Hessel. Situated on Nunn's Creek, where it enters Lake Huron, the site offers the tribe a chance to establish its own hatchery and to enhance fish supplies according to its own needs. Building a fishery around salmon could prove a serious mistake, since eating these predator fish and their eggs may entail substantial health risks. We do not know for sure. But the basic concept of an autonomous Indian fishery is a wise one, which would allow the Indians an opportunity to run their own affairs as they have not been able to do since the early nineteenth cntury. Nevertheless, even with these changes, most Chippewa and Ottawa fishermen will remain poor until the tribes make some specific provision for them.[7]

CHAPTER TEN
Epilogue

Conflicts similar to the dispute over Chippewa and Ottawa fishing rights will continue to flare up, mostly in the form of treaty-right litigation. Indeed, a new round of hostility has already erupted between whites and Indians in the Great Lakes region.

On February 18, 1987, Federal District Judge James C. Doyle (Western District of Wisconsin) ruled that the Chippewa Indians of Wisconsin and the western part of the Michigan upper peninsula could hunt, fish, and gather throughout their historic lands. Doyle granted access to many natural resources—the list fills three and a half double-spaced pages—and he scarcely restricted the place or method of harvest. If the Indians can show economic need, Judge Doyle's decision appears to grant them virtually limitless opportunities to hunt, fish, and gather whatever they want, wherever they want.[1]

Wisconsin state officials and sportsmen's groups throughout the nation are aghast. The widely applicable decision sets important precedents. If it holds up (and it probably will), Indians have rights to hunt deer, bear, ducks, geese, hawks, eagles, songbirds, and other birds and mammals without regard to state regulations. They can catch whitefish, lake trout, walleye, northern pike, muskellunge, perch, and other fish, again without restriction by state law. And they can harvest any plants or plant by-products they wish, including wild rice, maple sugar, and hardwood and softwood trees. It is an extraordinarily broad definition of Indian treaty rights but one fully consistent with legal precedents.

Judge Doyle's decision has direct application to Michigan

Epilogue 153

Indians who used nearly identical resources and signed treaties similar to those endorsed by the Wisconsin Chippewa. When they wish, Michigan Indians will easily establish in court their rights to harvest any and all natural resources, free of state controls. A decision of this sort will stir widepread opposition, since it affects many people and involves such a variety of resources. More people and interests will take action this time than was the case with Great Lakes fishing.

In the past, whites have typically confused such conflicts by immersing them in ideology and rhetoric. Witness the name-calling that went on during the Michigan treaty fishing dispute, when Indians were called environment-wrecking "supercitizens," who claimed to be above the law, and sportsmen and state officials demanded that everyone be treated equally as guaranteed under the Constitution. They mistakenly defined the Great Lake fishing controversy as an ecological issue involving conservation, not allocation, of fish. For the most part, such descriptions provoked misunderstanding and slowed the search for equitable resolution, however much popularity they brought to administrators, politicians, and leaders of sportsmen's groups, who used anti-Indian feeling to advance their careers.

Of course, the Great Lakes fishery does involve important environmental issues, just as do the resources involved in Judge Doyle's decision. Fish stocks must be protected. Pollution must be curbed and, wherever possible, water quality improved. Environmental constraints must be respected. These issues do not divide Indians and non-Indians but are shared by them. Neither monopolizes environmental wisdom or stupidity. Both have thoughtlessly misused the natural world, and neither has much right to claim virtue or call the other names. The name-calling ought to stop and the conflicts seen for what they are: matters of allocation and property rights.

Historically, property rights to Great Lakes fish have followed the logic of a free-access common-property system that suited the interests of outsiders and middlemen, benefited the big fishermen, and doomed the little fishermen to poverty. For the moment, the Chippewas and Ottawas have allowed such a system to continue in their fishery, though they seem ready to make some changes. Often seen as an outgrowth of natural conditions, this common-property system is, in fact, a social creation. Made by human beings, it can just as easily be unmade—adjusted to meet different needs from those served by a common-property system. We have seen how other fisheries have been organized in many ways to suit many purposes. Property rights to Great Lakes fish can easily be changed, if people want to change them.

Nor should we see the Great Lakes sport fishery as the ecologically proper way to organize the fishery so it serves all the people, the general public as it were. The Great Lakes sport fishery allocates the fish to people with leisure time and benefits entrepreneurs who operate tourist-related businesses. A system of allocation, the sport fishery is ecologically neither sound nor unsound.

Keeping in mind the limits imposed by environmental constraints, how should the Great Lakes fishery be allocated? Who should get the fish? Who the spin-off benefits? For that matter, how should the renewable resources that the Doyle decision makes available for Indian harvest be divided? Enhancement seems to provide the easy solution: increase supplies so that enough exists to meet the needs of all users. But typically resources cannot be increased enough to meet everyone's demands. Enhancement usually provokes ecological difficulties and often promises more than it can possibly deliver. Enhancement seldom, if ever, solves allocation difficulties. Hard choices have to be made, for in any system some people will gain and some will lose. It is that simple and that complex.

Defined in this fashion, the questions become political and their answers relative, not absolute, and contingent upon ethical considerations. Proper and not-so-proper allocation becomes a function of values. Different values produce dif-

Epilogue

ferent allocations, each "correct" as long as it abides by ecological constraints.

Of many potential criteria, the state of Michigan has chosen profit maximization as its standard. Moneymaking seems a reasonable basis for organizing the state-run fishery, provided the lure of profits does not lead officials to ignore the well-being of the fish, the waters, and the health of the people. Surely public health ought to take precedence over profit.

The Indian tribes have also committed their fishery to profit maximization. This choice seems equally reasonable for the tribes, but they need to take other criteria into account. The Sault tribe has initiated a wise course with its effort to assume full control of a put-grow-take salmon fishery in northern Lake Huron, provided the salmon are fit to eat. Indian control is the critical matter, and the Sault tribe and the others also need to control wholesaling and retailing if they are to realize the full benefits of the fishery. The tribes should establish wholesale and retail operations in northern Michigan and should at least explore the possibility of setting up Indian-run stores in major American cities.

Large profits could be made in an urban fish store. Americans are likely to continue to expand their consumption of fish, barring revelation of new health hazards, and fish should be a growth industry. But urban living threatens Indians who must separate themselves from family and community. The tribes would be wise to set up urban enclaves—colonies if you will—where fish store managers and employees could live among other Indians while doing a short-term stint in the city before returning to their rural or small-town homes. A vertically integrated fish business such as this, in which Chippewas and Ottawas controlled everything from hatcheries to urban retail stores, would greatly increase the benefits to Indians and, from their point of view, that would be a good thing, too long in coming.

Notes

Introduction. Rights, Resource Allocation, and the Fishery

1. See Christopher Vecsey and Robert Venables, eds., *American Indian Environments* (Syracuse, N.Y., 1980); Calvin Martin, *Keepers of the Game: Indian-Animal Relationships and the Fur Trade* (Berkeley, Calif., 1978); and Calvin Martin, ed., *The American Indian and the Problem of History* (New York, 1987).

2. Similar changes took place in New England. See William Cronon, *Changes in the Land* (New York, 1983).

3. Stanford H. Smith, "Species Succession and Fishery Exploitation in the Great Lakes," Contribution no. 368, Ann Arbor Biological Laboratory, U.S. Bureau of Commercial Fisheries.

Chapter One. The Fur Trade

1. Jacqueline Peterson, "Many Roads to Red River: Métis Genesis in the Great Lakes Region, 1680-1815," in Jacqueline Peterson and Jennifer S.H. Brown, eds., *The New Peoples: Being and Becoming Métis in North America* (Lincoln, Neb., 1985), 37-71.

2. Lyle M. Stone and Donald Chaput, "History of the Upper Great Lakes Area," *Handbook of North American Indians* (Washington, D.C., 1978), 15:602-9.

3. James M. McClurken, "Augustin Hamlin, Jr.: Ottawa Identity and the Politics of Persistence," in James Clifton, ed., *Being and Becoming Indian* (Chicago, 1989), 82-111.

4. Lewis Cass to John C. Calhoun, June 17, 1820, quoted in Henry R. Schoolcraft, *Narrative Journal of Travels through the Northwestern Regions of the United States . . . in the Year 1820*, ed. Mentor L. Williams (East Lansing, Mich., 1953), 317-18.

5. Henry R. Schoolcraft, *Personal Memoirs of a Residence of Thirty Years with the Indian Tribes on the American Frontiers* (Philadelphia, 1851), 458, 504-5.

6. See McClurken, "Augustin Hamlin, Jr." for an elaboration of Ottawa plans.

Notes to Pages 10-21

7. Antoine de la Mothe Cadillac, "Relation on the Indians," as cited by Vernon Kinietz, *The Indians of the Western Great Lakes* (Ann Arbor, 1972), 239.

8. Johanna E. Feest and Christian F. Feest, "Ottawa," *Handbook of North American Indians* 15:774-75, 780-81. See also James E. Fitting, *The Archaeology of Michigan*, rev. ed. (Bloomfield Hills, Mich., 1975), 195-97.

9. John Tanner, *A Narrative of the Captivity and Adventures of John Tanner* (New York, 1830), 36-39.

10. Andrew J. Blackbird, *History of the Ottawa and Chippewa Indians of Michigan* (Ypsilanti, Mich., 1887), 33.

11. Alexander Henry, *Travels and Adventures* (Ann Arbor, Mich., 1966), 95-96, 147, 125.

12. Ibid., 149.

13. Imre Sutton, *Indian Land Tenure* (New York, 1975), 23.

14. Eric R. Wolf, *Europe and the People without History* (Berkeley, Calif., 1982), 158-94.

15. Johann Kohl, *Kitchigami* (Minneapolis, 1956), 421.

16. Ruth Landes, "Ojibwa of Canada," in Margaret Mead, ed., *Cooperation and Competition among Primitive Peoples* (New York, 1937), 87-126.

17. George Boyd, Report on the Indians within the Agency of Michilimackinac, July 30, 1819, Mackinac Indian Agency, Letters Received, vol. 1; Petition to Andrew Jackson, [?] 15, 1835, Mackinac Indian Agency, Letters Sent, 77.

18. Charles E. Cleland, "The Inland Shore Fishery of the Northern Great Lakes: Its Development and Importance in Prehistory," *American Antiquity* 47 (1982): 761-84.

19. Francis Audrain to Henry Schoolcraft, June 13, 1833, Mackinac Indian Agency, Letters Received, 2:48-49; Schoolcraft to Major M.V. Cobb, September 23, 1835, Mackinac Indian Agency, Letters Sent, 121.

20. George Manypenny and Henry Gilbert to Secretary of Interior, August 7, 1855.

21. George Johnston to Henry R. Schoolcraft, June 20, 1833, Mackinac Indian Agency, Letters Received, 2:60; see also the petition sent to Schoolcraft in late May 1833, which can be found in Mackinac Indian Agency, Letters Received, 41.

22. Harold Demsetz, "Toward a Theory of Property Rights," *American Economic Review* 57 (May 1967): 347-59.

23. Frank G. Speck, "Land Ownership among Hunting Peoples in Primitive America and the World's Marginal Areas," *22nd International Congress of Americanists* (Rome, 1926) 2:323-32.

24. Eleanor Leacock, *The Montagnais Hunting Territory and the Fur Trade*, American Anthropological Association Memoir no. 78 (1954), 7.

25. Imre Sutton briefly reviews the literature on family hunting territories in *Indian Land Tenure*, 193-96.

Chapter Two. The Great Lakes Fishery, 1836-1965

1. Erhard Rostlund, *Freshwater Fish and Fishing in Native North America* (Berkeley, Calif., 1952).
2. Helen Tanner, "Fishing: The Important Occupation," in her *Report* (April 1974), *United States v. Michigan* M26-73 C.A., 34-47.
3. Grace Lee Nute, "The American Fur Company's Fishing Enterprise," *Mississippi Valley Historical Review* 12 (March 1926): 483-503.
4. Abel Bingham to James Ord, September 25, 1846, National Archives Microcopy 234, Roll 771.
5. James Ord to William A. Richmond, November 7, 1848, National Archives Microcopy 234, Roll 771.
6. Hugh M. Smith and Merwin-Marie Snell, *Review of the Fisheries of the Great Lakes in 1885* (Washington, D.C., 1889).
7. James W. Milner, *Report on the Fisheries of the Great Lakes* (Washington, D.C., 1873), 14-15.
8. Edward P. Allen to the Commissioner of Indian Affairs, August 24, 1883, in the *Annual Report of the Commissioner for 1883* (Washington, D.C., 1884).
9. The following discussion is based on an analysis of the United States Census of Population for 1860, Mackinac County. The census is available on microfilm from the Center for Research Libraries, Chicago.
10. Data are from the United States Census of Manufacture for Michigan, 1850 and 1870. The census may be found in the state archives.
11. Smith and Snell, *Review,* 67.
12. Smith and Snell, *Review,* 44, 91, 64, 61, 33.
13. Smith and Snell, *Review,* 211.
14. See Smith and Snell, *Review,* 31-185, for a description of the fishery's organization.
15. Milner, *Report,* 14.
16. Smith and Snell, *Review,* 78-79.
17. Smith and Snell, *Review,* 44.
18. James M. Acheson, "Variations in Traditional Inshore Fishing Rights in Maine Lobstering Communities," in Raoul Anderson, ed., *North Atlantic Maritime Cultures* (New York, 1982), 261. The Japanese inshore fishery, in which communal ownership was the rule, offers interesting comparisons. See Arne Kalland, *Shingu: A Study of a Japanese Fishing Community* (London, England, 1984). Maine lobstering seems analogous to the inshore Great Lakes fishery in that clearly identifiable

grounds remained productive year after year. Lobstering did not lend itself as easily to highly capitalized operations using elaborate technologies. John Cordell has collected articles on fish and property systems in *A Sea of Small Boats* (Cambridge, Mass., 1989). See esp. Peter R. Knutson, "The Unintended Consequences of the Boldt Decision," 263-303.

19. Kent O. Martin, "Play by the Rules or Don't Play at All: Space Division and Resource Allocation in a Rural Newfoundland Fishing Community," in Anderson, *North Atlantic Maritime Cultures*, 277-98.

20. Interview with William Carlson, January 1985; Walter Koelz, *The Fishing Industry of the Great Lakes*, U.S. Fish Commission (Washington, D.C., 1926).

21. Smith and Snell, *Review*, 60.

22. Legault and Kuchenberg, *Reflections*, 30-31.

23. Interviews with Ed Dutcher and Charles Williams. I was an eyewitness to the Ludington conflicts in August 1983. See also the People's Brief and the Opinion, *People of the State of Michigan* v. *Henry Felix Krawczyk*, District Court for the County of Mason, no. 83-CR-7949.

24. Data are from the United States Census of Population for Mackinac County, 1850-80. I estimated geographic mobility by comparing the names of fishermen listed in 1860 with the names listed in 1870 and assumed that those fishermen who were not listed in the later census had moved away. On the role of the middle class in preserving communal stability, see Robert Doherty, *Society and Power: Five New England Towns, 1800-1860* (Amherst, Mass., 1977).

Chapter Three. Social Structure and the Forests

1. Anita Shafer Goodstein, *Biography of a Businessman: Henry W. Sage, 1814-1897* (Ithaca, N.Y., 1962); Ruth B. Bordin, "A Michigan Lumbering Family," *Business History Review* 34 (Spring 1960): 64-76; and Martin D. Lewis, *Lumberman from Flint: The Michigan Career of Henry H. Crapo, 1855-1869* (Detroit, 1958).

2. Rolland Maybee, "Michigan's White Pine Era," *Michigan History* 43 (December 1959): 417-22.

3. Norman J. Schmaltz, "The Land Nobody Wanted: The Dilemma of Michigan's Cutover Lands," *Natural Resources Register* 3 (June 1983): 4-12.

4. William N. Sparhawk and Warren D. Brush, *Economic Aspects of Forest Destruction in Northern Michigan*, Technical Bulletin no. 92, U.S. Department of Agriculture (Washington, D.C., 1929), 11.

5. Report quoted ibid., 90.

6. George Blackburn and Sherman L. Richards, Jr., "A Demographic

History of the West: Manistee County, Michigan, 1860," *Journal of American History* 57 (December 1970): 600-618; George W. Hotchkiss, *History of the Lumber and Forest Industry of the Northwest* (Chicago, 1898).
  7. Blackburn and Richards, "Demographic History."
  8. Sparhawk and Brush, *Economic Aspects*, 19-20.
  9. Ibid., 70.
  10. Horace J. Andrews and William S. Bromley, *Trends in Land Use in Northern Michigan* (Washington, D.C., 1941), 16-17.
  11. *Forest and Stream*, June 18, 1874, 290, as quoted by James A. Tober, *Who Owns the Wildlife?* (Westport, Conn., 1981), 72.
  12. Ibid., 43.
  13. Elisha J. Lewis, *Hints to Sportsmen* (Philadelphia, 1851), quoted ibid., 46-47.
  14. Tober, *Who Owns the Wildlife?* 53.
  15. James B. Trefethen, *An American Crusade for Wildlife* (New York, 1975), 72.
  16. Tober, *Who Owns the Wildlife?* 95.
  17. Eugene T. Petersen, "Wildlife Conservation in Michigan," *Michigan History* 44 (1960): 129-46; idem, "Michigan Sportsmen's Association," *Michigan History* 47 (1963): 355-72.

Chapter Four. Tourism and Sport Fishing

  1. George W. Lee to Commissioner of Indian Affairs, August 1880, as quoted by Helen Tanner, *Report*, April 1974, *United States v. Michigan*, 28-29.
  2. I examined federal census records, 1850-80, for the counties in northwest lower Michigan and the eastern upper peninsula. Because of federal mismanagement, the Indians did not obtain title to land allotted under the Treaty of 1855 until the 1870s. In the Grand Traverse area, the Native Americans acquired fee-simple ownership in 1872, and most of them sold their land before 1880. It may be that none of these properties appeared on the censuses. I reviewed the census data carefully but did not analyze them statistically. See William J. Gribb, "The Grand Traverse Bands' Land Base: A Cultural Historical Study of Land Transfer in Michigan," Ph.D. diss., Michigan State Univ., 1982.
  3. William J. Gribb, "The Grand Traverse Bands' Land Base"; Bruce Rubenstein, "Justice Denied: Indian Land Frauds in Michigan, 1855-1900," *Old Northwest* 2 (1976): 131-40.
  4. George W. Lee to the Commissioner of Indian Affairs, August 31, 1876, National Archives Microcopy 234, Roll 411.

Notes to Pages 53-61

5. See Richard White, "Ethnohistorical Report on the Grand Traverse Ottawas," 107-38, unpublished manuscript which may be found in the National Indian Law Library, Boulder, Colorado; Bruce A. Rubenstein, "Justice Denied: An Analysis of American Indian–White Relations in Michigan, 1885-1889" (Ph.D. diss., Michigan State Univ., 1982); and Tanner, *Report*, 21-33.

6. Pamela J. Dobson, *The Tree That Never Dies: An Oral History of Michigan Indians* (Grand Rapids, 1978); U.P. Hedrick, *The Land of the Crooked Tree* (New York, 1948).

7. For the effects of tourism, see Northwest Regional Planning and Development Commission, "Overall Economic Development Plan," mimeo, 1978, Sec. 4, pp. 1-37, hereafter cited as OEDP. I obtained a copy from the Commission in its Traverse City office. Another copy may be found in the Traverse City Public Library. Two carefully researched monographs should also be consulted: Robert W. Marans et al., *Waterfront Living: A Report on Permanent and Seasonal Residents in Northern Michigan* (Ann Arbor, 1976); and Robert W. Marans and John D. Wellman, *The Quality of Nonmetropolitan Living: Evaluations, Behaviors, and Expectations of Northern Michigan Residents* (Ann Arbor, 1978).

8. Computed from *Michigan Statistical Abstract for 1977* (Lansing, Mich., 1979), 38-41.

9. Paul R. Voss and Glenn V. Fugitt, *Turnaround Migration in the Upper Great Lakes Region* (Madison, Wis., 1979).

10. I interviewed real estate agents in Harbor Springs, Charlevoix, Traverse City, and Beulah. See also OEDP, secs. 4, 5.

11. OEDP, secs. 4, 5.

12. Ibid., sec. 4.

13. Ibid. Personal observations. I have lived among the poor of northern Michigan.

14. Bernard R. Smith, "Sea Lampreys in the Great Lakes of North America," reprinted by the Great Lakes Fish Commission from *The Biology of Lampreys* (New York, 1971).

15. Vernon C. Applegate, "The Sea Lamprey in Michigan," *Michigan Conservation* 12 (July-August, 1949): 14-15.

16. Stanford H. Smith, "Species Interactions of the Alewife in the Great Lakes," Transactions of the American Fish Society 99 (1970): 754-765. Edward H. Brown, "Population Biology of Alewives . . . in Lake Michigan, 1949-1970," *Journal of Fisheries Research Board of Canada* 29 (1972): 477-500.

17. Jim Legault and Tom Kuchenberg, *Reflections in a Tarnished Mirror: The Use and Abuse of the Great Lakes* (Sturgeon Bay, Wis., 1978), 60-67; Great

Lakes Fishery Commission, *Annual Report for 1973* (Ann Arbor, Mich., 1974).

18. Legault and Kuchenberg, *Reflections*, 76-87; Wayne H. Tody and Howard A. Tanner, "Coho for the Great Lakes," *Fisheries Management Report* no. 1; "Michigan's Trout and Salmon Fishery, 1967-1972," *Fisheries Management Report* no. 5. Published by the Michigan Department of Natural Resources, these reports may be obtained by contacting the public information office of the DNR.

19. Gale C. Jamsen, "Sportfishing Activity in 1971," *Fisheries Management Report* no. 5; John Scott and Howard A. Tanner, testimony, January 13, 1978, U.S. House of Representatives, *Hearings Before the Subcommittee on Fisheries and Wildlife* (Washington, D.C., 1978), 138-80.

20. Howard A. Tanner, Testimony, House, *Hearings*, 138-64.

21. Daniel R. Talhelm and Paul V. Ellefson, "Economic Evaluations of the Fishery," Ellefson, "Economic Appraisal of the Resident Salmon and Steelhead Sport Fishery of 1970," both in *Fisheries Management Report* no. 5, 44-82; and Talhelm et al., *Current Estimates of Great Lakes Fisheries Values: 1979 Status Report* (Ann Arbor, Mich., 1979).

22. Phone conversation with Daniel Talhelm, November 1984.

23. Phone interview with Claude ver Duin, publisher and editor of the *Fisherman*, and Commissioner on the Great Lakes Fishery Commission, February 1981.

24. Personal observations. Also Harrison K. Osoinach, "Indian Politics and Culture in Rural Northern Michigan" (Ph.D. diss., Univ. of Michigan, 1976).

25. Beatrice Anne Bigony, "Migrants to the City: A Study of the Socioeconomic Status of Native Americans in Detroit" (Ph.D. diss., Univ. of Michigan, 1974); "Anthropological Report on the Grand Traverse Band," mimeo, a copy of which may be found in the genealogical collection of the Grand Traverse Band.

Chapter Five. Chippewa and Ottawa Treaty Rights

1. American Friends Service Committee, *Uncommon Controversy* (Seattle, 1970).

2. Jondreau testimony, *State of Michigan* v. *William Jondreau*, Baraga Cir. 33. Also Mich. App. 3585 and 384 Mich 538.

3. Interviews with Ottawa leader and treaty right fisherman, Arthur Duhamel, April 1981, January, August 1982.

4. Interviews with Director of Upper Peninsula Legal Services, William James, April 1980, and Albert LeBlanc, the most influential treaty right fisherman, May 1980.

Notes to Pages 70-79   163

5. See John F. Salan, "A Legal and Factual History of the Indian Fishing Problem in Emmet County, Mich.," in House *Hearings, January 13, 1978* (1978), 208-17.

6. Based upon personal observations of the Tribal Conservation Court at Bay Mills.

7. Between 1980 and 1985. I often fished with tribal fishermen. I acted as a guard for their trucks and trailers.

8. Personal observations based largely upon conversations overheard at fisheries in Mackinaw City and St. Ignace, Michigan.

9. My observations on the fishery are drawn from personal experience and listening to fishermen's conversations in the wholesale fisheries and bars in the Mackinac Straits area.

10. See the testimony presented January 13, 1978, House, *Hearings* (1978), esp. Mort Neff on behalf of Save Our Bay, 236-37; and the memorandum presented by Richard M. Zehner, president Grand Traverse Area Sport Fishing Association, 238-242; "The Need for U.S. Congressional Intervention to Re-establish Domestic Order and Tranquility in the State of Michigan, mimeo, January 13, 1978.

11. Interviews with tribal fishermen, primarily from the St. Ignace area. I observed Native American fishing in these areas between 1979 and 1985.

12. Charles M. Forster, Opinion, in *Grand Traverse Area Sport Fishing Association* v. *Clarence Maudrie et al.*, Circuit Court for Grand Traverse County, 79-510-CE.

13. John A. Scott, affidavit, August 22, 1979. Scott's affidavit is part of the trial record of *GTASFA* v. *Maudrie et al.*, cited in note 12 above.

14. Myrl Keller, Affidavit, August 25, 1979. Keller's affidavit is part of the trial record of *GTASFA* v. *Maudrie et al.* cited in note 12 above.

15. Phone interview with Josephine Bailey who filed a protest with the Suttons Bay school board after her children were harassed. June 1982.

16. See the *Northwoods Call* for the sportsman's view of the controversy.

17. See Traverse City *Record Eagle*, June 25, July 14, Dec. 7, 1977; Petoskey *News Review*, Oct. 10, 1975, June 6, 1977, Feb. 27, 1976, all quoted in John A. Fellows, "The Indian Gill-Netting Controversy in Michigan, 1971-1977" (Senior Honors Thesis, Univ. of Michigan, 1978).

18. Ben East, "They're Taking Your Fish, *Fishing the Midwest* (Spring 1979), 66-67, 140-42.

19. *Northwoods Call*, April 4, 1979.

20. *Northwoods Call*, April 18, 1979.

21. *Northwoods Call*, August 9, 1978.

22. Interview with John Alexander, August 1983.
23. Personal observations. I attended this meeting.
24. Traverse City *Record Eagle*, April 20, 1979.
25. *Northwoods Call*, May 2, 1979.
26. Interviews with Arthur Duhamel, Ron Paquin, and John Alexander, Summer 1980. Duhamel, Paquin, and Alexander are Indian fishermen.
27. Interviews with Dwight Lewis, former Director of Michigan Indian Legal Services. May 1980, April 1981, and Grand Traverse Band attorney, William Rastetter, May 1981.
28. Traverse City *Record Eagle*, April 21, 1979.
29. *Northwoods Call*, March 31, 1981; Traverse City *Record Eagle*, April 17, 1982.
30. Traverse City *Record Eagle*, April 17, 1982.
31. Grand Traverse Area Sport Fishing Association Newsletter, May 12, 1983.
32. Traverse City *Record Eagle*, June 28, 1983.

Chapter Six. Treaty Rights in the Courts

1. The following discussion is based primarily upon *United States* v. *Michigan* trial transcripts.
2. Charles J. Kappler, *Indian Affairs, Laws, and Treaties* (Washington, D.C., 1904), 2:729.
3. Ibid., 2:451.
4. Ibid.
5. Helen Tanner quoting Schoolcraft in Trial Testimony, 204.
6. Tanner, testimony, 215.
7. Taylor, opening statement, 1207.
8. Noel Fox, Opinion, 471 F. Supp. 192 (1979), 240-42.
9. See Elizabeth Neumeyer, "Michigan Indians Battle against Removal," *Michigan History* 55 (Winter 1971): 275-88.
10. Feest and Feest, *Handbook of American Indians* 15: 778-79; Peter Dougherty, "Diary," *Journal of the Presbyterian Historical Society* 30 (1952): 95-114, 175-92, 236-52; Blackbird, *History of the Ottawa and Chippewa*; Henry R. Schoolcraft, *Historical Condition and Prospects of the Indian Tribes of the United States* (Washington, D.C., 1847), vol. 1.
11. Philip Mason, testimony, 1559.
12. Ibid., 1835.
13. Fox, Opinion, 219.
14. Ibid., 200-202.
15. Ibid., 202.
16. Fox, Declaratory Judgment and Decree, May 7, 1979;

17. Interviews with William James, April 1980, and Albert LeBlanc, May 1980.
18. Fox, Opinion, *U.S.* v. *Michigan,* 16.

Chapter Seven. State Efforts to Regain Control

1. Based upon personal observation of vigilante activities and interviews with Ottawa and Chippewa fishermen and Gordon Peterson, a non-Indian fish wholesaler.
2. See *Michigan Out-of-Doors* 33 (January 1979): 15.
3. Traverse City *Record Eagle,* December 15, 1981.
4. Ibid., May 9, 1980.
5. Conversations with charter captains in Frankfort, Michigan. I observed gillnetting in the Grand Traverse Area, 1980-84. Reports of tests to determine lake trout supplies can be found in House, *Hearings,* 170-80. See also the affidavits of John Scott and Myrl Keller in *Grand Traverse Area Sport Fishing Association* v. *Clarence Maudrie et al.*
6. William Milliken to Ronald Reagan, as quoted in the Sault Ste. Marie *Evening News,* January 28, 1981.
7. Traverse City *Record Eagle,* June 6, May 2, 1980; Detroit *Free Press,* June 15, 1980.
8. *Evening News,* September 5, 1979.
9. Ibid., May 5, 1982.
10. Ibid., May 14, 1980.
11. Interviews with Sault tribe chairman, Joseph K. Lumsden, May 1982, and several conversations with Ron Paquin and Arthur Duhamel, both of whom negotiated for their groups.
12. *Record Eagle,* June 14, 1980.
13. Phone interviews with John Scott, January 1985.
14. Ronald Reagan to attorney Ted Swift, as quoted in the *Record Eagle,* October 31, 1980.
15. Quoted from the Traverse City *Record Eagle,* October 31, 1980.
16. *Record Eagle,* August 14, 1980.
17. *Federal Register,* April 28, 1980; Supplemental Brief of the Plaintiffs-Intervenors-Appellees to the U.S. Court of Appeals for the Sixth Circuit, 79-1527, 79-1528, 79-1414.
18. Supplemental Brief of Intervenor-Appellant Grand Traverse Area Sport Fishing Association to the U.S. Court of Appeals for the Sixth Circuit, 79-1527, 79-1528, 79-1414.
19. Detroit *Free Press,* April 16, 1981.
20. *Record Eagle,* April 21, 22, 1981; Detroit *Free Press,* April 26, 1981 (see the Tom Opre column).
21. James Watt to Grand Traverse Band Chairman, Joseph G. Raphael,

April 21, 1981. Watt sent identical letters to the chairman at Bay Mills and the Sault tribe along with the governor of Michigan.

22. Bruce R. Greene to Kenneth Smith, acting assistant secretary for Indian affairs, February 23, 1981.

23. Emergency Motion [of the State of Michigan] to Modify Stay and Request for Immediate Consideration (April 30, 1981) submitted to the U.S. Court of Appeals for the Sixth Circuit. See Bruce R. Greene's response in supplemental Brief of Plaintiffs-Intervenors-Appellees.

24. Detroit *Free Press*, May 10, 1981.

25. Supplemental Brief of Plaintiffs-Intervenors-Appellees, 26-33.

26. Phone interview with William P. Horn, February 1987. For the most part I have relied upon the handwritten notes of William Rastetter, attorney for the Grand Traverse Band; my personal observations; and a variety of informal conversations with participants as the basis for my descriptions of negotiations between 1981 amd 1985.

27. Personal observations. I attended the rally in Manistee on April 29, 1982. Watt's plan is described in the Traverse City *Record Eagle*, May 8, 1982.

28. Phone interview William P. Horn, February, 1987.

29. Detroit *Free Press*, May 30, 1982.

30. *Leelanau Enterprise*, April 8, 1982. For a typical Kelley outburst, see the Traverse City *Record Eagle*, December 15, 1981.

31. Detroit *Free Press*, May 30, 1982.

32. Phone interview with William P. Horn, February 1987; interviews with Nancy Kida, attorney for Michigan Indian Legal Services, August 1982.

33. Agreement in Principle (mimeo), copy in my possession.

34. *Evening News*, August 25, 1982; *Leelanau Enterprise*, August 26, 1982; Joseph Raphael and Arthur Duhamel to William Horn, September 10, 1982. Copy in my possession.

35. Phone interview with William P. Horn, February 1987. William Rustem signed the agreement for the state, "subject to clarification of unresolved questions and concurrence of the Department of Natural Resources, Governor and Attorney General."

36. Elmer T. Nitzsche, field solicitor, to Stewart Freeman, Dan Green, Wade Teeple, and Dr. Joe Kutkuhn, January 28, 1983.

37. Indian Tribes' Amended Motion to Allocate Resource.

38. See Richard A. Enslen to Attorneys of Record, June 28, 1984; Also Bruce R. Greene's response to Enslen, July 10, 1984, in which Greene suggests that no fisheries expert was needed.

Chapter Eight. With Utmost Good Faith?

1. Agreement for Entry of Consent Order, March 28, 1985.

Notes to Pages 124-134

2. *Legal Times*, April 22, 1985, 1, 8-10.
3. See McGovern's comments in the *Legal Times*, October 14, 1985, 2, where he warns that special masters are not scrutinized and may fall victim to improprieties.
4. William P. Horn, testimony, *United States* v. *Michigan*; Francis McGovern, "Report of Activities . . . from February 1 to March 10, 1985," copy in my possession.
5. Joseph K. Lumsden, Testimony, *U.S.* v. *Michigan*.
6. Francis E. McGovern, "Toward a Functional Approach for Managing Complex Litigation," *University of Chicago Law Review* (Spring 1986): 462.
7. I spoke with most of the important negotiators subsequent to their involvement in the March 1985 meetings. None of these men and women knew anything about the Lake Wasota Fishing Rights Game or any other computer simulation.
8. William Rastetter, notes, in his possession.
9. Phone interview with Elizabeth Valentine, April 1985; conversations with Greg Bailey and William Rastetter, May 1985; Phone interview with William P. Horn, February 1987.
10. McGovern, "Toward a Functional Approach," 440-93.
11. Ibid., 466-67.
12. Agreement for Entry of Consent Order, sec. 9. Copy in my possession. See also *U.S.* v. *Michigan*, Dispute Resolution Mechanism (mimeo).
13. I attended executive council meetings during the fall, 1986.
14. Agreement for Entry of Consent Order, sec. 2, p. 15.
15. McGovern, "Toward a Functional Approach"; Elizabeth Valentine, quoted in *Legal Times*, April 22, 1985, 10.
16. McGovern, "Toward a Functional Approach," 447.
17. I do not wish to denigrate Raphael's political skills, but they were much better suited to his Ottawa and Chippewa constituents than to the other "key decision makers."
18. Personal observations. I interviewed the negotiators, other than Skoog and the Parrishes. I did not attend the Sault negotiations, but I did observe other gatherings, formal and informal, during discovery.
19. Charles E. Cleland and Richard Bishop, "An Assessment of the Bay Mills Indian Community, Sault Ste. Marie Tribe of Chippewa Indians, and Grand Traverse Band of Ottawa and Chippewa Indians, and a Cost-Return Analysis of Treaty Commercial Fishermen-1981" (mimeo), April 1984. Copy in my possession.
20. The estimates are based upon personal experience. I operated a fish business in northern Michigan between 1982 and 1986.
21. Between 1985 and 1989, the tribal catch increased substantially, but

the larger and better capitalized fishermen were taking most of the fish, according to William Rastetter, whom I interviewed in August 1989.

22. Peter Steketee, "Position of MUCC on Allocation Issues," March 19, 1985. Copy in my possession.

23. As of 1989, eating salmon remains a potential health risk, but a market has opened for them during a brief late summer, early fall season.

24. William Eger, "Memorandum on the Impact of the Agreement on the Performance of the Treaty Fishery," December 5, 1986.

25. Ibid.

26. The following discussion is based on trial transcripts of *U.S. v. Michigan*.

27. *Win Awenen Nisitotung*, March 1986, 10.

28. Trial transcript, *U.S. v. Michigan*, 4-7.

29. William P. Horn, trial testimony, *U.S. v. Michigan*.

30. Noel P. Fox, Opinion, *U.S. v. Michigan*, 280-81.

Chapter Nine. What Should Be Done?

1. John Cordell, "Introduction: Sea Tenure," in John Cordell, ed., *A Sea of Small Boats* (Cambridge, Mass., 1989), 1-32.

2. *Federal Register*, June 29, 1979, 38329-40; *Evening News*, August 14, 1981, November 28, 1981; Detroit *Free Press*, July 6, 1989; Detroit *News*, June 30, 1989.

3. C. E. Johnson, et al., *Getting the Most from Your Great Lakes Salmon* (Madison, Wis., 1974); Ronald W. Rybicki, "A Summary of the Salmonid Program (1969-1970)," in *Fisheries Management Report* no. 5.

4. Wayne Schmidt, "Are *Your* Fish Safe to Eat?" *Michigan Out-of-Doors* 35 (September 1981): 36-37, 53.

5. Conversations with Grand Traverse band attorney, William Rastetter, and Chippewa fisherman, Ron Paquin, May 1987.

6. Personal observations. While operating a wholesale fish business, I hauled whitefish from St. Ignace to other cities in northwest lower Michigan.

7. Tribal plans for reorganizing the fishery are described in the newsletter of the Great Lakes Indian Fish and Wildlife Commission, *Masinaigan*. See the July 1987 issue.

Chapter Ten. Epilogue

1. Doyle's successor, Judge Barbara Crabb has upheld Chippewa treaty rights despite widespread opposition to them. The controversy can be followed in *Masinaigan*.

Index

alewives, 59-60, 142
Alexander, John, vii; quoted, 80-81
allocation of resources: among Native Americans, 2-3, 10, 15, 21-22; among whites, 47-50
alternative dispute resolution, 124-39; problems of, 125, 131, 132-33, 139
Andrus, Cecil, 111, 112
Ann Arbor agreement, 120-22; as basis for consent order, 125
annual round 7, 11-15

Bailey, Gregg, 127, 131
band organization among Native Americans, 15-16
Bay Mills Indian community, 69, 73, 75, 133, 136-37, 149, 150; resists consent order, 136-37
Benedict, Judge Richard L., 68, 83
big boat–small boat allocation, 34, 134-39, 149-50, 151
Blanchard, James, 122, 145

Carter, Jimmy, and his administration, 107, 110, 117
Cass, Lewis, 8
Cleland, Charles, 87, 88-89, 90, 94; reports on economic status of Indian fishermen, 133-34, 136, 137
Clifton, James, 87, 93-94, 96
commercial fishing, 24-32, 58, 65-66; profits, 26-27, 30-32; and community structure, 28-30, 36-37; by Indians, 25-26, 97-98; home waters and property systems in, 32-34; vigilantism in, 34-35
conservation, a surrogate allocation, 78, 84-85, 142, 153
contamination of predator fish, 136, 142-47, 155
Cordell, John, 141

Davis, Robert, 108
Department of Natural Resources (DNR), 39, 54, 58, 61, 63, 64, 65, 70, 72, 74, 76, 78, 81, 82, 83, 102-04, 108-09, 129, 143, 144, 145-46; confined by its ideology, 103, 108, 116, 153; conflict of interest in, 144-45
Dingell, John, 107, 113
Doyle, Judge James C., 152-53
Duhamel, Arthur, vii, 68

East, Ben, presents sportsmen's view of treaty fishing, 76-78
economic benefits of sport fishing, 64-65, 106-07

Eger, William, 136
Enslen, Judge Richard A., 117, 122-23, 124, 125, 132, 137, 138

Feest, Johanna and Christian, migration after the Treaty of 1836, 96-97
Forster, Judge Charles, 74, 81
Fox, Judge Noel, 79, 89, 96-102, 103-04, 105, 108, 109, 113, 114, 117, 123, 139
Freeman, Stuart, 120-21, 145

generosity among Chippewa and Ottawa, 2, 9-10
gill-net fishing and lake trout, 74-75
Grand Traverse Area Sport Fishing Association (GTASFA), 73, 81-82, 83-84, 112, 114, 118, 119
Grand Traverse Band of Chippewa and Ottawa Indians, 69, 73, 75, 121, 122, 133, 148, 149
Grand Traverse Bay, 73, 74, 115, 132
Great Lakes fishery, 8-9, 22-37, 58-66; and Indians, 10, 16-20, 23-29, 87-89; and American Fur Company, 18-19, 24-26; reorganization and technological change, 26-27, 29-31; value of, 63-64; absence of local control in, 34-37
Greene, Bruce R., vii, 69, 86-97, 101-102, 110, 112, 113, 114, 117, 118, 120, 122, 127, 131, 132, 137, 138

Hammond Bay, 135, 150
Henry, Alexander, 12-14
home waters, 32-35
Horn, William P., vii, 118-22, 124, 125, 127, 131, 132, 138, 143; negotiates Ann Arbor agreement, 120-22; sets basis for consent order, 124-25
hunting territories, 16, 20-22

Indian removal and fishing rights, 91-99

James, William, vii, 68
Jannetta, James, 97, 112
Jondreau, William, 67-68, 103

Keller, Myrl, 70, 74-75, 81
Kelley, Frank, 102, 105, 120
Kohl, Johann, 14-15
Kutkuhn, Joseph, 118

lake trout, 8, 32, 59, 61, 62, 65, 68, 70, 71, 72, 74-75, 76, 77, 79, 106-07, 108, 114, 116, 136, 142, 143, 146-47; impact of treaty gill-net fishing on, 74-75
Lake Wasota Fishing Rights Game, 125, 126-27
Landes, Ruth, 15
Leacock, Eleanor, 20-21
LeBlanc, Albert "Big Abe," vii, 68, 69
Lee, George W., 51-52
loss of land among Chippewa and Ottawa, 52-53
lumbering, 38-47; benefits leave the region, 3-4, 41-43; ecological impact, 38-41; and community structure, 40, 45; and Native Americans, 53-54
Lumsden, Joseph K., vii, 110, 120, 126, 127, 131, 132, 137

McElroy, Scott, 138
McGovern, Francis E., 123, 124-33

Index

market hunting, 38, 47-50
Mason, Philip, 95-99
Memorandum of Understanding (on fishing rules), 111, 112-13, 115
Michigan United Conservation Clubs (MUCC), 103, 105, 109, 135, 138, 144, 146
middle class and community stability, 36-37, 44-45; impact of export economy, 38-47; and geographic mobility, 36-37, 44-45
Milliken, William, 78, 81, 102, 106-07, 113, 115, 117, 118, 119-20, 146
mobility of Indian fishermen, 71-72, 75

Native American Rights Fund, 69, 137
newspaper and magazine accounts of treaty fishing, 75-79

Opolka, Frank, 109
ownership of resources among the Chippewa and Ottawa, 3, 12-22

Parrish, Arnie, Jr., 127, 131
Parrish, Irma, 127, 131
Pelt, Andy, 109
People v. LeBlanc, 68-69, 70, 71, 113, 114
population change and tourism, 55-56
poverty: among fishermen, 28-29, 36; among Native Americans, 51-53; in north woods after lumbering, 4, 40, 45-46

Raphael, Joseph, 127, 131, 167 n. 17

Rastetter, William, vii, 121
Reagan, Ronald, and his administration, 107, 109, 110, 111, 113, 117, 118, 138
rural to urban migration of Native Americans, 66

Salan, John, 70-71
Salmon (coho and Chinook), 61-62, 77, 106-07, 136, 142, 143, 145, 146-47, 155
Sault Ste. Marie agreement, 124-39
Sault Tribe of Chippewa Indians, 69, 73, 137, 148, 149, 150-51, 155
Schoolcraft, Henry R., 8, 9, 17, 92, 97
Schultz, Steve, 113, 117, 118, 119, 122
Scott, John, 74, 76, 83, 109
sea lamprey, 58-61, 142
Sheppard, Glen, the *Northwoods Call*, and treaty fishing, 78-79, 82
Skoog, Ron, 125, 127, 131, 132
social structure in northern Michigan, 38-50
Sparhawk, William N. and Warren D. Brush, report on economic impact of lumbering, 40-41; suggest decentralized economy to retain benefits, 45-46; encourage local self-sufficiency, 45-47
Speck, Frank G., 20
sport fishery, 58-66; benefits of, 63-66, 147; rejuvenated, 5, 51, 61-62
Steketee, Peter, 89, 94, 102, 135
Stop Gill Netting Association (SGN), 81-82

Swift, Theodore (Ted), 73, 112, 113, 114, 117, 118, 119
Tanner, Helen, vii, 87, 89-90, 91, 92, 96
Tanner, Howard, 61, 63, 102, 109, 113, 114, 115, 116-17, 143
Taylor, Gregory, 88, 89, 94-98, 102, 103-04
tourist economy, 2, 4-5, 51, 56-58, 63, 66; and long-time residents, 57-58; and Native Americans, 66
tourism, 39-40, 46-47, 54-58; and allocation of resources, 54-55; and sport fishing, 63-64
Treaty of 1820, 8, 17-18, 87, 90
Treaty of 1836, 8, 17, 68, 87, 89-97, 100-101
Treaty of 1855, 52, 87, 89-97, 100-101
treaty right fishing, 67-85

United States v. Michigan, 69, 86-104, 112, 123, 124, 137, 143
upper class hunters, 47-50
Upper Peninsula Legal Services, 68, 69

Valentine, Elizabeth, 117, 127, 130, 131, 145
Vander Jagt, Guy, 111-12, 113, 114, 115
vigilantism, 33-35, 73, 79-85, 105

Washington, Thomas, 109, 138
Watt, James, 112, 113, 114, 116, 118, 120, 138, 143
whitefish, 8, 17, 61, 70, 135, 137, 142
wholesalers of fish, 26, 31-32, 148
wild animals: ownership of, 47-50

www.ingramcontent.com/pod-product-compliance
Lightning Source LLC
Chambersburg PA
CBHW032047150426
43194CB00006B/445